GOMER
MESHECH
TOGARMAH
TUBAL
ASSHUR
(MEDES
ELAM
SHINAR
(BABYLONIA)
ARAM
CANAAN
DEDAN

Record of Revelation: The Bible

OTHER BOOKS IN THE SERIES

Record of the Promise: The Old Testament
Record of the Fulfillment: The New Testament

Record of Revelation

THE BIBLE

WILFRID J. HARRINGTON, O.P.

Foreword by Roland de Vaux, O.P.

THE PRIORY PRESS • CHICAGO, ILLINOIS

NIHIL OBSTAT: *Very Rev. Gilbert J. Graham, O.P.*
   Censor Librorum

IMPRIMATUR: ✢*Most Rev. Cletus F. O'Donnell, J.C.D.*
   Administrator, Archdiocese of Chicago
   May 8, 1965

*The Bible text in this publication is from the
Revised Standard Version of the Holy Bible,
copyrighted 1946 and 1952 by the Division of
Christian Education, National Council of Churches,
and used by permission.*

Library of Congress Catalogue Number 65-19356
© *Copyright 1965 by* THE PRIORY PRESS
*2005 South Ashland Avenue, Chicago, Illinois 60608
Manufactured in the United States of America*

Foreword

The Bible is both historical and doctrinal, containing the revelation which God made to men through his own deeds and words. The Bible tells the history of our salvation, the gradual unfolding of the divine plan of redemption all through the two Testaments or Covenants, first in the Old Covenant concluded between God and Israel and maintained by God in spite of the unfaithfulness of his Chosen People, and then in the New Covenant, open to all mankind and sealed by the blood of a son of this people who was also the Son of God. Moreover, the Bible shows how each man must enter into this Covenant and abide within it, thus achieving his personal salvation. It tells us what we must know about God and Man, and what man must do to become acceptable to God.

This word of God is meant for each one of us as it was meant for our remote ancestors in the faith. It is the source of our faith, as it was of theirs. To reach man and transmit the message of salvation, this word became "incarnate," even as the Word of God became flesh to achieve man's salvation. God's word became "the Book," or rather "the Books" of the Bible. And just as the Word made flesh took upon himself our entire human condition, except for sin, so too God's word was subject to the conditions of human language, except for error. It was transmitted through human authors in whom divine inspiration suppressed none of the traits which belonged to them as men of their own times, of their own environment, and of their own culture. These distinguishing characteristics vary from one sacred author to another, and they are different from ours.

The writing of the books of the Old and New Testaments took place during a period of a thousand years, and the last of these books was written nearly two thousand years before our day. During these three thousand years, the face of the world has changed many times. God spoke to the ancient Israelites in the language of their time, and he spoke differently to those who came out of Egypt with Moses and to those who returned from the Exile with Esdras. Jesus spoke to the Jews of his day. And we are different from both the ancient Israelites and from the Jews of the time of Christ. Biblical writers who received and transmitted the sacred message were Semites who thought and spoke like Semites. Our thinking is not the same as theirs and we speak in different terms.

The Church was constituted by God as the guardian and interpreter of the word; but the Bible, considered as a book which contains that word, has not been preserved from the accidents that affect the transmission of any human text. It was copied, and the copyists made mistakes or introduced changes. It was translated, and the translators were not always accurate. It was expounded, but the commentators did not always understand it very well. In spite of all this, the message of the Bible is everlasting and is valid for all men of all times and all places. Indeed, the Bible has always been the most widely read book in the world, and men of the most diverse origins find the teaching of truth and a rule of life in its pages. It is because the Bible comes from God that it has this universal human value, and bears within itself the grace of light for all men of good will.

However, the mystery of the divine message itself and the dissimilarity of the times and concepts of those who first transmitted it and those who receive it today constitute serious obstacles. The Bible reveals its full richness only through the combined work of the exegete and the theologian, and since the Bible's richness is inexhaustible, this task is never finished. There will always be efforts to find a purer text or a more accurate translation, or to understand it better by placing it again within the human context in which it was first written, and to penetrate more deeply its divine meaning by the light of faith. Even as meditation on the life and deeds of Jesus will never elucidate the whole mystery of his Person, the study of the Bible will never quite exhaust the content of God's word.

Biblical study is a duty for every student who makes use of holy Scripture in developing his own theology, or who seeks his spiritual nourishment within it, and who will be preaching it to the faithful. It is also of interest to the laity who have acquired a taste for holy Scripture because of the biblical revival of our time and who now participate more intimately in the liturgy of the Word as the result of recent reforms. Both groups need to be introduced to this study and guided in this reading. It is for both of them that Father Harrington has written these three volumes on the record of revelation. It is a pleasure to be able to say that he has admirably achieved his purpose. He has clearly delineated a sound theological introduction to the entire Bible. He has made use of the conclusions best established by modern research in introducing the books of both the Old and New Testaments. Readers will readily see how these positions established by biblical science accord with the mind of the Church, the guardian of the Bible. By following this guide, they will proceed from the books of the Promise to the books of the Fulfillment, and the written word will give them a better knowledge of the Word Incarnate, "Jesus Christ, the focal point of both Testaments, of the Old as its hope, of the New as its model, and of both as their core" (Pascal).

Roland de Vaux, O.P.
Harvard University
Easter, 1965

\Preface

After some years of teaching experience, I am more conscious than ever that we lack an introduction to the Bible in English that might form the basis of a Scripture course for students of the Bible. At the same time, there is no fully-satisfactory work that may be recommended to interested layfolk. It would be presumptuous to claim that this introduction fills both needs, or either of them, but it is an attempt to grapple with these· needs. It is designed as a textbook which will provide the student with a clearly-defined foundation and will leave the professor a little more time to get on with the essential task of expounding the text of the Bible. Since it is meant to be self-explanatory, or largely so, it is hoped that it may also serve as a "teach yourself" book for those who do not have the advantage of a professor. Such, at least, are the aims, and time alone will show whether or not they have been attained.

When I say that no suitable work is available, I am not disdaining the admirable *Guide to the Bible*.[1] Yet it will be admitted, I believe, that this work can rather bewilder the student, who prefers to have the matter presented more succinctly and arranged more systematically. The *Guide* (or its French original, *Initiation Biblique*) has been supplanted by the massive two-volume *Introduction à la Bible*[2]

---

[1] A. Robert and A. Tricot, *Guide to the Bible*, trans. E. P. Arbez and M. R. P. McGuire (New York: Desclée, 1960[2]), I-II.

[2] A. Robert and A. Feuillet, *Introduction à la Bible* (Tournai: Desclée, 1957-59), I-II.

ix

—easily the best introduction to the Bible by Catholic scholars. The reader will quickly observe that I have leaned heavily on this splendid work. I think I can say that, as a consequence, this introduction to the Bible faithfully presents the views of some of the finest biblical scholars of our day.

The most important section of the whole introduction is formed by Chapters Three to Six of this first volume, which treat inspiration, inerrancy, and the senses of Scripture. In these chapters I have been content to follow exclusively one who is an acknowledged authority in this field: Father Pierre Benoit, O.P., professor at the École Biblique and editor of the *Revue Biblique*. Father Benoit has, over the years, built an imposing synthesis. I believe that the more profitable approach—the alternative would be to present and evaluate different opinions—is to place this synthesis before the student. He can be sure that every step has been carefully worked out by a master. Other solid opinions will be found in the Appendix at the end of this book, and will be indicated in the footnotes and Bibliography.

It remains for me to thank Father Thomas C. Donlan, O.P., of The Priory Press who commissioned this work; without his invitation and encouragement I should never have undertaken it. I owe a special debt of gratitude to my colleagues, Fathers Liam G. Walsh, O.P. and Thomas P. McInerney, O.P., professors at St. Mary's, Tallaght, Ireland, for their painstaking reading of my manuscript and for their valuable criticism and suggestions.

I am grateful also to Father Kevin A. Lynch, C.S.P., who has kindly granted me permission to make free use of material in *What is the Bible?* published by the Paulist Press and copyrighted by the Missionary Society of St. Paul the Apostle.

W. J. H.

Table of Contents

Foreword   v

Preface   ix

Abbreviations of Sacred Scripture   xiv

ONE: *The Written Word*   3
  1. THE BOOKS OF THE BIBLE   4
  2. THE FORMATION OF THE BIBLE   6
     1) The Old Testament   6
     2) The New Testament   15
  3. THE BIBLICAL WRITINGS IN CHRONOLOGICAL ORDER 16

TWO: *The Word of God to Men*   20
  1. THE TWO INCARNATIONS   20
  2. THE PEOPLE OF THE WORD   21

THREE: *The Inspired Word*   25
  1. THE FACT OF INSPIRATION   25
     1) The Testimony of Scripture   25
     2) The Testimony of the Fathers   26
  2. ERRONEOUS VIEWS ON INSPIRATION   27
  3. REVELATION AND INSPIRATION   29
     1) Revelation in the Bible   30
     2) Inspiration in the Bible   32
  4. SUMMARY   34

FOUR: *The Psychology of Inspiration*   35
  1. DEFINITION OF INSPIRATION   35

2. PRACTICAL JUDGMENT AND SPECULATIVE JUDGMENT   36
3. REVELATION, INSPIRATION, AND JUDGMENT   38
4. HOW THE INSPIRED WRITER IS MOVED   39
5. THE EXTENT OF INSPIRATION   43

FIVE: *The Inerrant Word*   46
1. THE EXTENT OF INERRANCY   46
2. THE INTENTION OF THE SACRED WRITER   48
3. INERRANCY AND HISTORY   49
4. LITERARY FORMS   51

SIX: *The Senses of Scripture*   54
1. SECONDARY SENSES   55
2. FULLER SENSE AND TYPICAL SENSE   56
3. CONDITIONS AND CRITERIA OF THE SECONDARY SENSES   59
4. THE SECONDARY SENSES AND INSPIRATION   61
5. A NOTE ON THEOLOGICAL CONCLUSION AND ACCOMMODATION 62

SEVEN: *The Canon of Scripture*   63
1. CANON AND CANONICITY   63
2. DEUTEROCANONICAL AND APOCRYPHAL BOOKS   64
3. THE FORMATION OF THE CANON   65
    1) *History of the Canon of the Old Testament*   65
    2) *History of the Canon of the New Testament*   68
4. THE CRITERION OF CANONICITY   72
5. APPENDIX: THE QUMRAN SCROLLS   73
    1) *Discovery of the Scrolls*   73
    2) *The Qumran Library*   74
    3) *The Essenes of Qumran*   78

EIGHT: *The Text of the Bible*   80
1. THE LANGUAGES OF THE BIBLE   80
    1) *Hebrew*   80
    2) *Aramaic*   81
    3) *Greek*   81
2. THE MANUSCRIPTS   82
    1) *Hebrew*   82
    2) *Greek: New Testament*   84
3. THE GREEK AND LATIN VERSIONS   93
    1) *The Septuagint (LXX)*   93
    2) *The Versions of Aquila, Theodotion, and Symmachus* 95
    3) *The Old Latin Versions (it)*   96
    4) *The Vulgate (vg)*   97

NINE: *Biblical Criticism*   102

1. TEXTUAL CRITICISM   103
   - 1) *Verbal Criticism*   103
   - 2) *External Criticism*   104
   - 3) *Internal Criticism*   105
2. LITERARY CRITICISM   106
   - 1) *The Language*   106
   - 2) *The Composition*   106
   - 3) *The Origin of a Writing*   108
3. HISTORICAL CRITICISM   109
4. THE BIBLE IN THE CHURCH   112
   - 1) *The Church and the Bible*   112
   - 2) *The Authentic Interpretation of Scripture*   113
   - 3) *The Biblical Encyclicals*   114
   - 4) *The Biblical Commission*   114
5. CONCLUSION   116

APPENDIX: *Karl Rahner and J. L. McKenzie on the Inspiration of Scripture*   119

Bibliography   133

General Index   137

ABBREVIATIONS USED FOR
THE BOOKS OF THE BIBLE

Gn.: Genesis
Ex.: Exodus
Lv.: Leviticus
Nm.: Numbers
Dt.: Deuteronomy
Jos.: Joshua
Jgs.: Judges
Ru.: Ruth
1,2 Sm.: 1,2 Samuel
1,2 Kgs.: 1,2 Kings
1,2 Chr.: 1,2 Chronicles
Ez.: Ezra
Neh.: Nehemiah
Tb.: Tobit
Jdt.: Judith
Est.: Esther
Jb.: Job
Ps(s).: Psalms
Prv.: Proverbs
Qoh.: Qoheleth
    (Ecclesiastes)
Ct.: Canticle of Canticles
Wis.: Wisdom
Sir.: Sirach
    (Ecclesiasticus)
Is.: Isaiah
Jer.: Jeremiah
Lam.: Lamentations
Bar.: Baruch
Ezek.: Ezekiel
Dn.: Daniel
Hos.: Hosea
Jl.: Joel

Am.: Amos
Obad.: Obadiah
Jon.: Jonah
Mi.: Micah
Na.: Nahum
Hb.: Habakkuk
Zeph.: Zephaniah
Hag.: Haggai
Zech.: Zechariah
Mal.: Malachi
1,2 Mc.: 1,2 Maccabees
Mt.: Matthew
Mk.: Mark
Lk.: Luke
Jn.: John
Acts: Acts
Rm.: Romans
1,2 Cor.: 1,2 Corinthians
Gal.: Galatians
Eph.: Ephesians
Phil.: Philippians
Col.: Colossians
1,2 Thes.: 1,2 Thessalonians
1,2 Tm.: 1,2 Timothy
Ti.: Titus
Phm.: Philemon
Heb.: Hebrews
Jas.: James
1,2 Pt.: 1,2 Peter
1,2,3, Jn.: 1,2,3, John
Jude: Jude
Ap.: Apocalypse

Record of Revelation: The Bible

THE BOOKS OF THE BIBLE
THE FORMATION OF THE BIBLE
THE BIBLICAL WRITINGS IN CHRONOLOGICAL ORDER

The Bible may be described as the collection of writings which the Church has recognized as inspired; often this collection is also called the Scriptures, Holy Scripture, the Sacred Books, and, especially, the Testament. The word "Bible" comes to us from the Greek via the Latin. The Greek expression is *ta biblia* ("the books"); in later Latin the borrowed word *biblia* (neuter plural in Greek) was taken to be a feminine singular Latin noun meaning "the book." Hence, for us, the Bible is the Book par excellence.

Although there is a true sense in which the Bible may be considered as one great work—the work of a divine Author—yet, from the human standpoint, it is not a book; it is not even *the* book; it is a library or, better still, it is the literature of a people, the Chosen People, God's people. This, as we shall see, is a very important observation, a fact that must be grasped if we are to have a proper understanding of the Bible.

We find that Scripture is divided into two parts: we speak of the Old Testament and the New Testament. The word "testament" is an approximate translation of the Greek *diathēkē;* it indicates a fundamental feature of revelation, the Covenant or treaty which God made with a people whom he had chosen, the people of Israel. This treaty (in Hebrew *berith*), which was renewed more than once, was also a contract, since the people too, on their side, accepted certain conditions, especially the obligation of being faithful to him, the one true God. The Old Testament is the story of this

3

people in the light of the Covenant, a story largely of infidelity on their part—inevitably bringing just punishment in its train—and of unfailing fidelity on the part of God.

God's purpose, the redemption of mankind, was to be achieved by sending his Son into the world. The coming of the Son of God naturally marked the beginning of a new era. God made a new and final treaty, sealed in the blood of Christ, with a new people —yet directly descended from the old—the Church. The New Testament tells of the fulfillment of God's plan. This plan, however, was there from the beginning, for the Testaments, although distinct, are closely linked. The Old Testament leads up to and is the preparation, God's preparation, for the New. Indeed, the Old Testament can be fully understood only in the light of fulfillment.

1. THE BOOKS OF THE BIBLE

The Jews, very wisely, had an elastic division of their Bible; they spoke of the Law, the Prophets, and the (other) Writings. The Law, which in their estimation took pride of place, consisted of the five books of Moses, the *Pentateuch*. Among the Prophets they listed not only the books that we term prophetical, but also Joshua, Judges, Samuel, and Kings, called by them the Former Prophets. Significantly, they did not number Daniel among the Prophets (as we do), but placed it in the third division, the Writings, which grouped the remaining books. The Hebrew division has much to recommend it, especially the fact that it does not (and this is particularly true of the Writings) seek to fit the various books into predetermined categories. We may indicate it more clearly thus:

The Law (*torah*): The Pentateuch.

The Prophets (*nebiim*)
{
Former: Joshua to Kings.
Latter: Isaiah, Jeremiah, Ezekiel, and the 12 minor prophets.
}

The Writings (*kethubim*)
{
1) Psalms, Proverbs, Job—the "great" writings.
2) Canticle of Canticles, Ruth, Lamentations; Qoheleth (Ecclesïastes), Esther—the "scrolls."
3) Daniel, Ezra, Nehemiah, 1, 2 Chronicles.
}

Since the thirteenth century, Catholics have divided the Old Testament into *historical, didactic,* and *prophetical* books. The division is a convenient one and does, in the main, give a good indication of the general character of the different books; but it must not be pressed too far because, in certain cases, it may be quite misleading. However, it will be useful to give a list of the biblical books according to this division.

1. *Historical*: The Pentateuch (Genesis; Exodus; Leviticus; Numbers; Deuteronomy); Joshua; Judges; Ruth; 1 and 2 Samuel; 1 and 2 Kings; 1 and 2 Chronicles; Ezra; Nehemiah; Tobit; Judith; Esther; 1 and 2 Maccabees.

It should be noted that in the Vulgate and Douay:

1,2 Samuel = 1,2 Kings
1,2 Chronicles = 1,2 Paralipomenon
Ezra, Nehemiah = 1,2 Esdras

but the names given in the list above are now almost universally accepted. Note further that since 1,2 Sm. = 1,2 Kgs. in the Douay, then 1,2 Kgs. in the list above = 3,4 Kgs. in the Douay.

2. *Didactic* (and poetical): Job; Psalms; Proverbs; Qoheleth (Ecclesiastes); Canticle of Canticles; Wisdom; Sirach (Ecclesiasticus).

3. *Prophetical*:

Four major prophets: Isaiah; Jeremiah (plus Lamentations and Baruch); Ezekiel; Daniel.

Twelve minor prophets: Hosea; Joel; Amos; Obadiah; Jonah; Micah; Nahum; Habakkuk; Zephaniah; Haggai; Zechariah; Malachi.

In Catholic versions of the Bible many of these names are usually spelled differently, and the same is true of most other proper names. The reason for this is simple. Proper names in the Douay are based on the Vulgate which, in its turn, has accepted the Greek forms of the names as they occur in the version of the Old Testament known as the Septuagint. The King James Version (1611), and all subsequent Protestant versions, have adopted the Hebrew form of the names. Conformity in this matter would be very welcome and there is a steadily growing movement among Catholics to accept the Hebrew forms.

The New Testament is sometimes, on the model of the Old, divided into historical, didactic, and prophetical books.

1. *Historical*: The Four Gospels; Acts of the Apostles.

2. *Didactic*: Epistles of St. Paul: Romans; 1,2 Corinthians; Galatians; Ephesians; Philippians; Colossians; 1,2 Thessalonians; 1,2 Timothy; Titus; Philemon. The Epistle to the Hebrews. The Catholic Epistles: James; 1,2 Peter; 1,2,3 John; Jude.

3. *Prophetical*: The Apocalypse.

2. THE FORMATION OF THE BIBLE

1) *The Old Testament*

The formation of the Old Testament was a lengthy process. Sacred history begins with God's choice of Abraham sometime during the nineteenth century B.C.; and the origins of the Old Testament, the traditions built around the patriarchs, go back in germ to Abraham, the man of the divine promises, and to his immediate descendants. But it was Moses, the born leader and the lawgiver, who, in the thirteenth century, forged a motley crowd of refugees into a nation, set on foot a mighty religious movement, and gave the impetus to the great literary achievement that is Israel's—and ultimately God's—gift to mankind.

The *Pentateuch* bears the stamp of Moses, but the work as we know it took its final form many centuries later than Moses: in the sixth or, more likely, in the fifth century B.C. The prophetical literature began with Amos and Hosea in the eighth century and closed with Joel and Zechariah 9-14 in the fourth century B.C. The historical books range from Joshua (based on traditions going back to the thirteenth century B.C.) to 1 Maccabees, written about the beginning of the first century. The fifth century, which saw the final form of Proverbs and the appearance of Job, was the golden age of the wisdom literature, but the movement had begun under Solomon in the tenth century, while the Book of Wisdom emerged a bare half-century before Christ. This is enough—even though nothing has been said of the complex genesis of individual books—to indicate that the shaping of the Old Testament was unhurried and involved.

We have to realize that most of the books of the Old Testament are the work of many hands, a work that has grown over a long period, perhaps over centuries. All who have collaborated in the production of each book, whether they have written the substance of it or have merely added some details, have been inspired. Most of them were quite unaware of being moved by God; hence for the moment we too shall consider the human side only of the Bible and view it as a collective effort, the work of a whole people which has deposited in the Bible, through the centuries, the treasures of its tradition. It is the literature of a people, enmeshed in the history of that people. We shall sketch briefly that literary activity from its beginnings and set it against its historical background; in this way we shall obtain a view of the Old Testament that will greatly facilitate our understanding of it.[1]

Much of the Old Testament is based on oral tradition. That part of it which comes first in our Bible—the *Pentateuch* to Samuel—is based on many oral traditions centered mainly around the patriarchs, Moses, Joshua, the Judges, Samuel, David, and later, in a section of Kings, Elijah and Elisha. These traditions, even before they were set down in writing, formed a true literature. "Literature" is, primarily, an art form; in a sense it is incidental that most literature has been set down in writing because, principally, it is a matter of words and language (whether written or not). Although, as we shall see, the biblical books as we know them took final shape at a relatively late date, this only marks the definitive setting down in writing of traditions that had begun, and in many cases had reached full development, many centuries before. The date of a biblical *book* is, very often, no indication of the date of the material contained in the book; and when we speak of "traditions" we do not exclude the possibility—indeed the certainty—that many of them may have been written down quite early. In fact, as will become clear, later literary activity in Israel was, to a large extent, concerned with the re-editing of earlier writings. We do not, then, by any means ignore or underestimate the contribution of previous centuries when we set the

---

[1]The date of a biblical book is generally difficult to establish. The dates given in this chapter are always approximate. However, within limits, there is a definite consensus in this matter among leading Catholic scholars of the day.

beginning of biblical literature, strictly understood, in the reign of Solomon.

In the face of Philistine aggression which, in the middle of the eleventh century, had overthrown the Israelite amphictyony (the confederation of twelve clans united in covenant with Yahweh), Israel made her first bid to organize herself as a monarchy. Despite initial promise, Saul proved a failure, but the idea of monarchy was not abandoned. A new beginning was made with David who succeeded in establishing a kingdom, and even a modest empire; a situation that was maintained and exploited by his son, Solomon. In order to handle the administration of kingdom and empire a class of scribes, educated men, emerged. Royal annals were kept and the business of state was recorded and filed away in archives. This provided the raw material of historical writing. Very early in the peaceful reign of Solomon (c. 970-931 B.C.) a writer of exceptional gifts produced the prose masterpiece of the Old Testament, the court history of David: 2 Sm. 9-20 and 1 Kgs. 1-2. A contemporary writer, of hardly less literary skill and endowed with a keener mind, working on old traditions, wrote a theology of history which forms one of the four main strands of the *Pentateuch*.[2] David (c. 1010-970 B.C.), whose skill as a poet is given abundant testimony, was the author of some of the psalms. These form the nucleus of the Psalter. The whole work, receiving its original impetus from him, was traditionally attributed to him. In quite the same way, the Wisdom literature, which developed in the following centuries, was attributed to Solomon, the proverbial wise man, who had begun the movement among the Hebrews or, at least, had provided the atmosphere for its emergence.

After the death of Solomon, the kingdom, united by David, broke apart, and Israel (or the Northern Kingdom) and Judah henceforth went their separate ways. A religious schism followed the political division, Judah alone remaining true, not only to the dynasty of David, but to a purer form of the authentic religion. In Israel one *coup d'état* followed on another and the worship of Yahweh—at the schismatic shrines of Bethel and Dan—was much affected by foreign

---

[2]The *Pentateuch* is a combination of at least four distinct traditions; literary analysis has unravelled the four strands.

influences. The Book of Kings gives us the parallel religious history
of the two kingdoms.

It was in Israel that Elijah and Elisha, the champions of Yahweh,
appeared; around them grew up the traditions that we find in 1
Kgs. 17–2 Kgs. 1 (Elijah) and 2 Kgs. 2-13 (Elisha). It was in
Israel too, during the reign of Jeroboam II (783-743 B.C.) that the
first of the so-called "writing" prophets, Amos and Hosea, carried
out their mission, even though Amos was a Judean. About the same
time, another strand of the *Pentateuch tradition,* parallel to the
Yahwistic tradition that had evolved in Judah, took definite shape.
This Northern tradition—in its final form the work of the Elohist,
as we now name this author—faced with the abuses in the worship of
Yahweh current in Israel, was understandably more conservative than
the other, setting up as its ideal the religion of the Exodus and of
the desert. Shortly after Amos and Hosea, the Prophets Isaiah and
Micah arose in Judah. However, only the first part of the Book of
Isaiah (i.e., chaps. 1-39)—and not even all of that—can be attributed
to this great Prophet of the eighth century. Isaiah himself tells us
of disciples who had gathered around him (8:16). It was these who
published his prophecies; the inspired writers who later added to
the work of their master came from that same school which continued
through the centuries.

Meanwhile, the terrible scourge of Assyria had begun to make
itself felt and the days of the Northern Kingdom were numbered.
Samaria, its capital, fell to Sargon II in 721 B.C.; the population of
the land, in accordance with Assyrian policy, was deported; and
Israel, as a separate entity, disappeared from history. Before the
final tragedy, some refugees, religious men who had seen the writing
on the wall, fled to Judah, taking with them their sacred traditions.
As a result of this, under Hezekiah (716-687 B.C.) the two earliest
strands of the *Pentateuch* (the Yahwistic and Elohistic traditions)
were combined. Another heritage of the North, brought to Jerusalem
at the same time, was the legislative part of Deuteronomy (the
deuteronomical code, Dt. 12-26). This was to have a powerful and
far-reaching effect—but not just yet.

The great power which had destroyed Israel menaced Judah too,
but the latter, thanks in great measure to the efforts of Isaiah, man-

aged to survive. A century later, Assyria, while apparently at its apogee, collapsed and disappeared with dramatic suddenness. In the short period that covered the decline of Assyria, before its successor the Neo-Babylonian Empire could assert itself, Judah was granted a brief respite and the young and pious king, Josiah (640-609 B.C.), was able to begin a religious reform. One of the first works to be undertaken was the restoration of the Temple—which had been sadly neglected—and during the work of renovation the "book of the Law" was discovered (2 Kgs. 22:8-10). This was the deuteronomical code which had been brought to Jerusalem by refugees from Israel one hundred years before and which had been deposited in the Temple, to be disregarded and eventually forgotten. Now providentially coming to light again, it became the charter of the reform and was published in the framework of a discourse of Moses; this first edition of the work corresponds to chapters 5-28 of our Deuteronomy. It was later re-edited during the Exile when the other discourses of Moses were added, one at the beginning and the other at the end.

Deuteronomy (or, more precisely, the first edition of it) gave the impulse to a very important literary work. The deuteronomical outlook was profoundly religious and striking in its singlemindedness: the nation stood or fell by its fidelity or unfaithfulness to Yahweh and to his Law. The history of the Chosen People was measured by this yardstick and the result provided the answer to a perplexing problem. The problem was this: on one hand stood the divine promises, which could not fail, and on the other hand one catastrophe after another had befallen the nation—Israel had disappeared and Judah had only just survived. The deuteronomists (as we may conveniently term them) saw very clearly that all these evils had come upon them because the people had been consistently unfaithful to their God; this was the one obvious lesson of their history. These men set about editing the older historical traditions, in the process giving to that history their own special religious slant. But they were careful not to do violence to the material, making their point either by means of modest insertions or by providing a distinctive framework. For example, in the Book of Judges the cycle of infidelity, punishment, repentance, and deliverance in which the story of each of the great Judges is set, is the work of these editors. During the reign of Josiah, the books Joshua-Judges-Samuel-Kings were edited, with Deuteronomy (chaps. 5-28) as an introduction. 2 Kgs. and Dt. were completed during the Exile (587-538 B.C.), and early in this period the history Joshua-Kings was edited for the second (and last) time. The Prophets Zephaniah and Nahum flourished during the reign of Josiah; Habakkuk was a little later than Nahum: both were contemporaries of Jeremiah.

After the untimely death of Josiah (609 B.C.), the Kingdom of Judah moved quickly to destruction; its last tragic years were reflected in the life and person of Jeremiah. The preaching of this great Prophet had gone unheeded—except to the extent that he had been persecuted for it—but after his death it had a profound influence. His message was recorded and published by his faithful disciple Baruch. In 587 B.C. Jerusalem fell to Nebuchadnezzar, as Jeremiah had emphatically declared it would, and its inhabitants were deported to Babylon. This must have seemed the end, but in God's unfathomable design the Exile was to be the crucible in which the religion of Yahweh was purified of all dross; it marks, too, a decisive moment in the formation of the Bible.

Side by side with the deuteronomical movement there was another, of which the Law of Holiness (Lv. 17-26) is representative. This movement was inspired by the outlook of the priestly class who insisted on the holiness of Yahweh and who pictured the nation as a priestly people whose whole life was a liturgy. Ezekiel, who had been transported to Babylon with other Judeans sometime before the fall of Jerusalem, probably in 598 B.C., was a product of this school; whereas his contemporary, Jeremiah, was more in the line of Deuteronomy. During the Exile, the priests, now cut off from the Temple and its cult, turned to the old traditions, especially to the Mosaic legislation, and edited and presented these from a marked cultic viewpoint. Almost all the legislation in Genesis to Numbers belongs to this tradition, although it includes much narrative besides; and, after the Exile, it was the priests who gave the *Pentateuch* its final form.

Not all Judeans had been deported; some few remained, and from time to time these came to weep over the ruins of the Temple. It was in these circumstances that Lamentations took shape. It is universally recognized that this is not the work of Jeremiah, although

the writing is attributed to him by the Vulgate—but not in the
Hebrew Bible. Baruch, placed immediately after Lamentations in
the Vulgate, is of uncertain date. In Babylon the exiles were com-
forted by an anonymous prophet, a late, but authentic, disciple of
Isaiah; his work, composed in the years before 538 B.C. (when Cyrus
the Great, having taken Babylon, permitted the Jews to return to
Palestine), is contained in Isaiah 40-55. These chapters mark a theological (and poetical) summit of the Old Testament. Very soon
after the return to Jerusalem, chapters 56-66 were added to Isaiah
by other members of the Isaian school. Nor was this the end, because
in the fifth century chapters 34-35 and 24-27 finally closed the work
that had begun in the eighth century. But with Second Isaiah (as
we name the unknown author of Is. 40-55) prophecy had reached
its climax; it would gradually decline, to disappear in the fourth
century, until the time of fulfillment.

The first of the exiles returned to Jerusalem from Babylon in
538 B.C.; eventually the Temple and the city were rebuilt. The work
of restoration was encouraged and supported by the Prophets Haggai
and Zechariah (only Zech. 1-8 belong to this period). Early in this
period—at the latest early in the fifth century—the Torah was finally
fixed. Deuteronomy, because it completed the story of Moses, was
detached from the great historical work (Joshua-Kings) and attached
to the first four books of the Bible. The *Pentateuch* came into being.
The little Book of Ruth was probably written soon after the return
(though it may possibly have appeared before the Exile). The last
of the prophets appeared in the fifth and fourth centuries: the
author(s) of Is. 34-35; 24-27; Mal.; Obad.; Joel; and the author of
Zech. 9-14.

At this time too, that is to say, in the fifth century especially,
another type of literature flourished: the wisdom literature. This
was not altogether new by any means, because already under
Solomon a practical outlook had found expression in sayings and
maxims governing everyday life. "By 'wisdom' one must understand
not only an encyclopedic knowledge of everything under the sun,
but also the concise definition of all forms of human behavior, in
particular the art of being the perfect gentleman. This art, so indispensable for the attainment of a successful career, had been

practiced for centuries in Egypt."[3] In Israel, however, this practical wisdom was, to a certain extent at least, always inspired by faith in Yahweh, a tendency very marked after the Exile. In the fifth century the Book of Proverbs (parts of which go back to the time of Solomon) took final shape and, shortly afterwards, the poetic masterpiece of the Bible appeared: Job.

The Book of Job is by no means the only poetical work in the Bible. In the first place there are the psalms: David undoubtedly composed some of these and the number continued to grow steadily. The building of the Second Temple (after the return from the Exile) and the re-establishment of the Temple cult, gave a new impetus to the composition of these liturgical poems and to the adaptation of older psalms. By the end of the fourth century it is very likely that the Psalter, as we know it, was complete. In that same century the Canticle of Canticles made its appearance.

The writing of history did not end with the Exile, and the restoration, dominated by the figures of Ezra and Nehemiah, found its historian too. The books 1, 2 Chronicles, Ezra, Nehemiah (four books in our Bible) really form only one volume, the work of a single author whom we conveniently call the Chronicler. In the first part of this writing (1, 2 Chr.) the author follows, to a large extent, the Books of Samuel and Kings. In the second part he depends on the memoirs of Ezra and Nehemiah and on other documents of the same period. The differences between 1, 2 Chr. and Sm.-Kgs. are marked because, whereas the latter is a religious history, the Chronicler has written a theology of history. Rather like the deuteronomists, he has drawn a religious message from the history of his people; but he uses that material much more freely than they. He wrote for his contemporaries and pointed out to them once again that the existence of the nation depended on its fidelity to its God; he would have his people be a holy community in which the promises made to David might at last be fulfilled. The work was written in the fourth century, just before the advent of Alexander the Great. Somewhat earlier, in the days of Ezra, and in opposition to a narrow nationalist outlook, the author of Jonah, a brilliant satirist, stressed the universal providence of God. And about the

---

[3]L. H. Grollenberg, *Shorter Atlas of the Bible,* trans. Mary F. Hedlund (Camden, N.J.: Nelson, 1959), p. 94.

same time the Book of Tobit, in form not unlike a modern novel, extolled the daily providence of God.

In 333 B.C., with Alexander's conquest of Syria and Palestine, the Greek period began in Judah. For the Jews, or for those at least who were faithful to their traditions, this meant, not the assimilation of Greek culture, as it did elsewhere, but resistance to the Greek way of life. An indication of this perhaps may be seen in the emergence of a typically Hebrew literary form, the *midrash*.[4] The form already influenced the work of the Chronicler, but it is early in the Greek period that we find the first developed biblical *midrash*. In this period also (about the middle of the third century) we may date Qoheleth (Ecclesiastes), and sometime afterwards, about 180 B.C., another wisdom writer, ben Sirach, wrote Sirach (Ecclesiasticus).

Soon the Jews had to face a great crisis. When Antiochus IV (175-163 B.C.) came to the throne of Syria, he determined to force his Jewish subjects to adopt the Greek way of life. The consequent religious persecution provoked the Maccabean revolt, which began in 167 B.C. Towards the close of the first part of the struggle (167-164 B.C.), the author of Daniel published his work in order to encourage his countrymen. The first part of the work (Dn. 1-6) is a *midrash*; and in Dn. 7-12 we find a perfect example of a Jewish literary form then in vogue: the apocalypse. Daniel appeared just before 164 B.C. (At a later date the book was supplemented by the addition of 3:24-90 and chapters 13-14.) Esther was written shortly after Daniel.

The last historical works of the Bible capture the spirit of the stirring Maccabean times. About the year 100 B.C., 1 Maccabees was published. 2 Maccabees, composed in Greek and adapted from the work of a certain Jason of Cyrene, is a little earlier, about 120 B.C. It covers much the same ground as 1 Mc. and, like it, it is a historical writing, but it is oratorical in style and tends to handle details with some freedom. The Book of Judith, a *midrash*, appeared early in the first century.

If the Palestinian Jews had effectively resisted Hellenization, some Jews in the important center of Alexandria successfully assimilated

---

[4]*Midrash* is a method of exegesis which developed rather late in Judaism; it is fully explained in W. F. Harrington, *Record of the Promise: The Old Testament* (Chicago: The Priory Press, 1965).

Greek thought without sacrificing their Jewish heritage. The last work of the Old Testament, the Book of Wisdom, was written by one of these. However, although it is a product of the Alexandrian school and was written in Greek, the Greek influence should not be exaggerated; its author was not a philosopher but an authentic "wise man" of Israel.

2) *The New Testament*

The New Testament differs from the Old in many important respects, but it is like the Old Testament in being closely linked to the life and development of a people, the new people of God: the early Church. Similarly, although the whole of the New Testament took shape within the first century of the Christian era, nevertheless its genesis is also complex. And just as the Jews regarded the five books of Moses, the Law, as the first and most important part of the Old Testament, so also Christians regard the four Gospels as the heart of the New Testament. These have their origin in the apostolic preaching, but the first three Gospels, as we know them, did not appear for a generation or more after the resurrection: Mark is dated 64-65 A.D., and Matthew and Luke to a time immediately before (or, perhaps, just after) 70 A.D.—the date of the destruction of Jerusalem by the Romans. St. Luke wrote the Acts of the Apostles soon after his Gospel.

In the meantime, between the years 51 and 67, St. Paul had written his epistles, or letters, to various churches, often dealing with special problems. In these epistles we find the beginning and the first development of our specifically Christian theology; reading between the lines we learn about the Christian life and the difficulties of the early Church. The Epistle to the Hebrews was written shortly before 70 A.D. by a disciple of St. Paul. James appeared in the year 50 A.D. or, more likely, in 58 A.D.; St. Peter wrote his epistle (1 Peter) about 64 A.D. Of the other "catholic" epistles (so-called because, for the most part, they are addressed to Christians in general) Jude and 2 Peter were written in the decade 70-80 A.D., and 2, 3 John, followed by 1 John, were written in the last decade of the century. Apocalypse, a book that is not quite as mysterious as it seems, in its final form dates from about the year 95 A.D. The most eventful century in history had nearly ended when the Fourth Gospel was published.

All that has been said about the formation of both Testaments is in no way irrelevant, but has a practical bearing on our study of inspiration. It is not merely (this concerns the Old Testament especially) that we cannot name the authors of most of the books; if the problem were simply this, it would not trouble us because we can say that the eventual author—whoever he may have been—was inspired. In practice, however, we can rarely point to any individual as the author of a whole book. We have remarked, for instance, that Isaiah contains material ranging from the eighth century to the fifth century. Our notion of inspiration must be supple enough to accommodate this situation and others like it.

It ought to be abundantly clear by now that the Old Testament is the ultimate result of a collective effort. The same is proportionately true of the New Testament, especially of the Gospels. The work of an evangelist was not a private undertaking; in reality he was the last link in a chain. The Gospel, founded on the works and words of Christ, was first lived in the Church; and the evangelist, although himself directly inspired by God, was also the spokesman of a Church guided by the Spirit of God. Thus the New Testament, no less than the Old, bears witness to the truth that God's written word, like his Incarnate Word, came quietly among us, growing and developing until the moment of its manifestation to men. The sacred writers were moved by the Spirit in a special way, but the long preparation which their labors crowned was all part of God's saving plan, his solicitude for his Chosen People, the Old Israel and the New.

3. THE BIBLICAL WRITINGS IN CHRONOLOGICAL ORDER

It is convenient to give a schematic view of the biblical writings, indicating the approximate date of each. The correct sequence, which will manifest the steady development within the Bible, is, of course, essential for an intelligent reading of Scripture.

With regard to the Old Testament books, the title "Other Writings" suggests that the works listed under that heading do not really belong to the categories in which they are traditionally placed. It is better, then, to list them apart, because each of them must be studied by itself and its particular literary form established. In the New Testament, the heading simply groups the writings that do not come under the other titles.

CENTURIES B.C.	HISTORICAL WRITINGS	PROPHETICAL WRITINGS
13th	Moses: Beginnings of *Pentateuch* literature. Joshua: Traditions of the Conquest.	
12-11th	Judges: Traditions of the Judges.	
10th	Solomon (c. 970-941) *2 Sm.* 9-20 and *1 Kgs.* 1-2. Yahwistic tradition fixed.	
9th	Elijah and Elisha Traditions underlying 1 Kgs. 17— 2 Kgs. 13. Elohistic tradition fixed.	
8th	Deuteronomical Code fixed.	*Amos* *Hosea* *Isaiah* (1-39) *Micah*
7th	Under Hezekiah (716-687), Yahwistic and Elohistic traditions combined. Under Josiah (640-609), first edition of *Deuteronomy* (Dt. 5-28). First edition of deuteronomical history, *Joshua-Kings.*	*Zephaniah* *Nahum* *Habakkuk*
6th	Before the Exile During the Exile (587-538) Second (and final) edition of *Deuteronomy.* Final edition of *Joshua-Judges-Samuel-Kings.* Priestly tradition fixed after the Exile.	*Jeremiah Ezekiel* *Lamentations* *Second Isaiah* (40-55) *Haggai; Zechariah* (1-8) *Isaiah* (1-39)
5th	*Pentateuch* fixed	*Isaiah* (34-35; 24-27) *Malachi* *Obadiah*
4th	*Chronicles-Ezra-Nehemiah*	*Joel* *Zechariah* (9-14)
3rd		
2nd	*2 Maccabees*	
1st	*1 Maccabees*	

CENTURIES B.C.	WISDOM AND POETICAL WRITINGS	OTHER WRITINGS
13th		
12-11th	David (c. 1010-970) Beginning of the *Psalms* Solomon	
10th	Beginning of *Wisdom* literature	
9th		
8th		
7th	Many Psalms	
6th		
5th	*Proverbs* *Job*	*Ruth* *Jonah* *Tobit*
4th	*Psalter* complete *Canticle of Canticles*	
3rd	*Qoheleth*	
2nd	*Sirach*	*Baruch* *Daniel* *Esther*
1st	*Wisdom*	*Judith*

NEW TESTAMENT WRITINGS			
A.D.	GOSPELS AND ACTS	EPISTLES OF ST. PAUL	OTHER WRITINGS
51		*1,2 Thessalonians*	
56		*(Philippians?)*	
57		*1 Corinthians* *1 Galatians* *2 Corinthians*	
57/58		*Romans*	
58 61-63		*(Philippians?)* *Colossians* *Ephesians* *Philemon*	*James*
64 64-65	*Mark*		*1 Peter*
65		*1 Timothy* *Titus*	*Hebrews*
67 68-70	*Matthew* *Luke* *Acts*	*2 Timothy*	
70-80			*Jude* *2 Peter*
90-100			*Apocalypse* *2 John* *3 John* *1 John*
	John		

TWO

The Word of God to Men

THE TWO INCARNATIONS
THE PEOPLE OF THE WORD

We believe that the Bible is the word of God, and so indeed it is. Yet no truth, perhaps, has been so often and so consistently misunderstood. Many still imagine that God speaks to us in every word of Scripture, just as he spoke to the contemporaries of Moses, of the prophets, or of the sages; to think so is to misconceive God's way of dealing with us. If God has condescended to speak to men, he has not only chosen to speak to them in the language of men, but has spoken to men in a language that could be understood by those to whom his word was first committed and by whom the Bible was written, under his inspiration. God does indeed speak to us, but through the people of the Old Testament and through the Christians of the first century.

1. THE TWO INCARNATIONS

Before going on to consider this capital truth, we must try to realize what is involved in the fact of God speaking to men. Perhaps the best way of grasping this is to follow the lead of the Fathers who have pointed to a parallel between the two incarnations of the Word of God: in human language and in human flesh. Just as we know that the Son of God became like men in all things, except for sin (Heb. 4:15), so also we can say that the written word of God is like human language in every way, except that it can contain no formal error. We can, indeed we must, push the parallel further. Christ is not only *like* men, he is truly Man and truly God; Scripture is not

20

only *like* human language, it is human language in the fullest sense, and all the while it is the word of God.

God speaks to us through human authors whom he uses and moves for that purpose. He moves them, as we shall see, in such a manner that they write only what he wills. We can be sure that we have grasped what God really means only when we are sure of the intention of the human writer, for it is through him, and not directly, that God addresses all the readers of his Scriptures. But there is more to it than that: God adapts his message to the talents of his chosen instrument and to the culture of those for whom the message was first intended. In the concrete, he has spoken to us, and still speaks to us, through the mouths, not of Europeans or Americans, but of ancient Semites. Here, too, the parallel with the Incarnate Word holds good, for Christ was not a Man of undetermined race or epoch, he was a Jew of the first century.

2. THE PEOPLE OF THE WORD

We may not ignore the human conditioning of God's word, under peril of misinterpreting God's message. More specifically, we must strive to understand and to appreciate the Semitic origin and the Semitic cast and background of the Bible, for all this is an essential part of it. We may not measure the Scriptures by our Western standards; rather, we should seek to understand the mentality of its writers. Obviously this calls for a certain reorientation. Western culture has its roots in Greece and Rome; the Greek heritage especially (although most of us may be unaware of it) has influenced our way of thought. We use abstract ideas and abstract terms, but the biblical writers, and our Lord himself, used concrete terms and imagery. Our manner of thought comes naturally to us, but we have to realize that the Semitic mind works differently; consequently Semitic outlook and culture are different from ours. We hasten to add that the Semitic manner of thought and expression in no way indicates any intellectual inferiority. The Greeks may have developed philosophy, but even here we have to be on our guard, for we do tend to equate philosophy as such with the product of Western thinkers. The Greeks have produced great literature, but the literary masterpieces of the Bible stand in the first rank of world literature. In the field of theology the Hebrews are supreme, but here again we betray our Western bias.

For us *the* theologians are men like Augustine and Aquinas, while the truth is, that until the end of time, we shall ever find new depths in the really great theologians of the Bible: the Yahwist, Job, Paul, John— to mention only the giants. We have more to learn from the Hebrews than we are willing to admit. Hence we should school ourselves to approach the Bible not only with the reverence that befits the word of God, but with the intellectual humility that recognizes in it an unsurpassed achievement of the human spirit.

At least, today we do know that the Semitic mentality was very different from the Greek. For one thing, a Hebrew did not, in the realm of knowledge, stress the primacy of speculative knowledge. For us, "to know" means to grasp an idea; for the Semite it involves much more than that. "Knowledge" of God, in biblical language, is not a speculative notion of God: it is a movement of the whole being, an involvement of a love governing the whole of life; it includes the acceptance of all that God stands for; it includes the service of God. One goes to God by obedience and service rather than by contemplation. In the Bible, "to hear" is more important than "to see," because perfection consists less in looking to the mystery of the divine essence than in listening to the appeals of God's love. Biblical religion is a religion of action much more than a religion of knowing.* Furthermore it is a fact that, in the eyes of the Semite, God is not an abstract essence, a pure spirit: he is Creator, Judge, Father. The very idea "pure spirit" does convey something to us; we understand, vaguely at least, that God is immaterial. To the people of the Bible the expression would be meaningless, because they did not have our distinction (which is entirely Greek) between spirit and matter. Nor did they speak of "soul" and "body" as we do; for them the whole man was the object of attention. Our more precise terminology has its dangers, even in the spiritual life. We speak of saving our "souls," as if our bodies were not to share in our sanctification and in our eternal fate; a wrong emphasis here frequently has led to an unchristian attitude towards material creation.

We are inclined to regard the Bible as a sort of textbook (if not, more reprehensibly, as a book of texts) in which we look for a set

*See Pierre Benoit, *Aspects of Biblical Inspiration*, trans. J. Murphy-O'Connor and S. K. Ashe (Chicago: The Priory Press, 1965), pp. 62-63.

of doctrines; and we are somewhat ill at ease because the teaching is not set down in logical order. What we should seek is the living image of a God who acts, who enters into our history, who speaks to our hearts; then we shall understand why the Old Testament can describe God as the Shepherd of his people: "I myself am the shepherd of my sheep" (Ezek. 34:15)—words that are echoed by the Son of God: "I am the good shepherd" (Jn. 10:11,14). We shall realize how it is that God can be presented as the Spouse of Israel: "Your Maker is your husband, the Lord of hosts is his name" (Is. 54:5); and how, in the New Testament, the Church is the Bride of Christ (Ap. 21:9). We have systematized the doctrines of the faith, and set them out in precise technical language, and thrown them into the form of a catechism—but Jesus taught in parables; he took striking examples from everyday life and spoke the language of poetry.

Of course, we do not seek to disparage systematic theology. One should keep in mind, however, that our theology, as a system, grew up later than the Scriptures. It has its roots in the Bible, in the New Testament especially, but it speaks another language; it translates the striking, often daring, images of Semitic speech into precise, carefully-framed formulas. In doing this it renders a necessary service; but we should not expect to find the same scientific terminology in the Scriptures any more than we ought to regard the Bible as a theological *treatise* (although, of course, it is *theology* from first to last). We lose the whole flavor of the word of God if we want to have its teaching parceled out in neat, clearly-labeled compartments. In short, we must strive to understand the Bible as it is and not try to force it into our categories of thought.

The Semitic cast is not confined to the Old Testament, but involves the New Testament also. Except for St. Luke, the New Testament writers were Jews. Even Luke is not really an exception, because in great part his writings are Semitic in tone. All four Gospels, in particular, have this quality; they are not speculative, but are always vivid and concrete—a fact which does not prevent the Fourth Gospel from being the most profound theological work ever written. In these Gospels we read of a Man who is the Son of God, who lived among us and taught and suffered and died and rose from the dead. He was born of the Jewish race and came and preached to Jews in the concrete, picturesque language of Semites; and the evangelists, although they wrote in Greek, were faithful to the Semitic culture that was theirs and his. It is this culture and outlook and way of speech that we must reckon with from one end of the Bible to the other—while not denying a certain Greek influence on some later books. If we persist in treating the Bible as a twentieth-century product of Western thought, we cannot fail to do it violence.

When we have once grasped this, our approach to the Bible will be along the right lines. If we do no more than realize that the mentality of the biblical writers is different from ours, we can begin to understand many aspects of the Bible that had hitherto puzzled us. We should also remember that the latest part of Scripture was written nearly two thousand years ago and that the earliest part of it took shape another thousand years or so before that. This is a further, obvious reason why the Bible can present difficulties: it is a product of its own time; hence we cannot hope to understand it as readily as we would a modern work. Besides, it has to be translated into modern languages before we can even begin to read it, because few people have an adequate knowledge of Hebrew (and Aramaic) and Greek.

Once again we must stress the important, fundamental truth that God has spoken to us *in human language*. The Bible is not only the word of God, it is also the word of men, and the human aspect of it is something we may not ignore. Our only way of knowing what God has to tell us in his Scriptures is by knowing first of all what the human writer has said. God has used him and moved him; in speaking to men, God has spoken by the mouth of a man whom he has chosen for that purpose. Only by listening carefully to that human voice can we catch the accents of God himself.

THE FACT OF INSPIRATION
ERRONEOUS VIEWS ON INSPIRATION
REVELATION AND INSPIRATION

An adequate notion of inspiration must apply to the Bible as it is in all its complexity; this is why we have dwelt on the origin of the Bible and its nature. Only now are we ready to examine the concept of inspiration itself.

1. THE FACT OF INSPIRATION

1) *The Testimony of Scripture*

There is no explicit mention of scriptural inspiration in the pages of the Old Testament, yet there are many passages which hint at it. We learn, for example, that it was at the divine bidding that Moses wrote the book of the Covenant (Ex. 24:4 f.; 34:27) and that Jeremiah set down in a book the oracles of the Lord (Jer. 30:2; 36:2). The Jews had a threefold division of their sacred books and they believed that all of them came from God. Thus the Law was regarded *as* the word of God while the Prophets *spoke* the word of God; these, with the Writings, constitute the "sacred books" indicated in 1 Mc. 12:9.

The Church inherited these Scriptures and accepted their sacred character. Our Lord had already referred to them and had cited them as the word of God (Mt. 22:31; Mk. 7:13; Jn. 10:34 f.) which must be accomplished (Mt. 26:54; Lk. 24:44 f.). The Apostles have done likewise: it is the Holy Spirit who spoke by the mouth of David, according to St. Peter (Acts 1:16; 4:25), and St. Paul said the very same of Isaiah (Acts 28:25). Arguments could be based on

25

Scripture as on divine authority (Rom. 3:2; 1 Cor. 14:21; Heb. 3:7; 10:15, etc.). Furthermore there are two classic texts, 2 Tm. 3:16 and 2 Pt. 1:21, which, with reference to the Old Testament, consider respectively the extent and the nature of inspiration.

In 2 Tm. 3:14 f., St. Paul exhorts Timothy to persevere in sound doctrine as befits one who has been instructed by the Apostle and has known the "sacred writings" from his childhood. The next verse goes on to say: "All Scripture is inspired by God and is useful for teaching, refuting, redressing, and for forming in justice." "All Scripture" (literally, "whatever has been written") is clearly the same as the "sacred writings" (cf. v. 15), that is to say, the whole Old Testament. It should be noted that the reading in the Douay Version— following the Vulgate—"all Scripture, inspired by God, is profitable . . ." is possible, but all modern scholars accept the other rendering. The Douay reading does indeed assert that Scripture is inspired, but it cannot be applied to the whole Old Testament as the other, and better, rendering can.

2 Pt. 1:21 points out that no prophecy can be the subject of private interpretation. Verse 21 adds: "A prophecy never came from a human will but, impelled by the Holy Spirit, men have spoken on the part of God." "Prophecy," mentioned in verse 21, is certainly the same as that "prophecy of Scripture" of its immediate context (v. 20), that is to say, the written prophetical word. We thus learn what prophecy is: the effect of a special movement of the Holy Spirit.

Both of these texts refer to the Old Testament only; there is no explicit testimony in Scripture to the inspiration of the New Testament, although some indirect arguments are commonly indicated. For example, in 1 Tm. 5:18 St. Paul cites as Scripture, that is, under the same heading ("Scripture says"), Dt. 25:4 and a saying of Christ found in Lk. 10:7. And in 2 Pt. 3:15 f. the epistles of St. Paul are set on a par with the other Scriptures which are certainly regarded as inspired.

2) The Testimony of the Fathers

The Church's belief in the divine inspiration of Scripture is clear, from the earliest times, in the tradition of the Fathers and in the teaching of theologians of all ages, quite apart from many special pronouncements.

The earliest Fathers, those of the second century, named the Scriptures the "oracles of God" which were "dictated by the Holy Spirit" who used the sacred writers as "instruments." Later writers (those of the third and fourth centuries) spoke of the Holy Spirit as the "author" of Scripture and asserted that both Testaments were inspired by the Holy Spirit. St. Augustine could describe the Bible as a letter from heaven; St. Jerome spoke of the sacred writer as an instrument of God; St. Gregory the Great went so far as to say that, since the Author of Scripture is the Holy Spirit, it does not matter who the human writer is. The teaching of the Fathers on inspiration may be summarized in two statements:

1. God (the Holy Spirit) is the author of Sacred Scripture.

2. The human writer is the instrument of God.

Along with this tradition of the Fathers we have a whole series of pronouncements on the part of the Church, in which may be traced a steady development and a growing precision. Until the fifth century the Church was principally engaged in defining and defending the extent and content of the word of God, and lists of the sacred books were drawn up. From the sixth century to the thirteenth century it was repeatedly stated that those books are sacred because God is their author and also, in view of certain heresies which minimized or rejected the Old Testament, that God is the one same Author of the Old Testament and of the New. At the Council of Florence (1441), a reason (found already in the Fathers) for this last statement was brought forward: God is the Author of both Testaments because the sacred writers of both Testaments have spoken under the inspiration of the same Holy Spirit. This was repeated by the Council of Trent and the First Vatican Council, the latter also making clear what inspiration is not. The encyclical *Providentissimus Deus* gives a positive definition of inspiration; certain aspects of inspiration are further developed in the encyclicals *Spiritus Paraclitus* and *Divino Afflante Spiritu*.

2. ERRONEOUS VIEWS ON INSPIRATION

The existence of inspiration is a dogma of faith; its nature, however, is a more complex matter, and not all theories of inspiration have done justice to it. Indeed some have been so defective that the

Church has had to step in and draw attention to their defects and even condemn them outright.

Among such theories, repudiated by the First Vatican Council, are those of *subsequent approbation* and *external assistance*. According to the former theory it was suggested that inspiration would be safeguarded if God, directly or through the Church, approved of, and declared immune from error, a book composed by unaided human industry—obviously, God would not be, in any sense, the author of such a book. In the theory of external assistance, inspiration was reduced to a mere negative help by which God preserved the writer from error—but again God is not the author of the book. Some non-Catholic theories are not very different. It is thought, for instance, that God is the author of the sacred books because he willed that they should be written; hence he chose suitable writers whom he commanded or prompted to write—once, again, all the work is theirs. Many current writers, then, reduce biblical inspiration to the level of poetic inspiration.

This is one extreme; it is to be expected that the other extreme was not always avoided. Often we find that the role of the sacred writer was minimized: he faithfully and mechanically wrote the things dictated by God and he was altogether passive, like a pen in the hand of a writer. This view obviously destroys human authorship. It is far removed from the true Catholic doctrine of inspiration. The First Vatican Council clearly presupposes human initiative when it rejects the opposite error: "not because (the sacred books) were composed by *human industry alone.*" It is true that phrases and images can be found in the early Fathers which, if pressed, seem to imply mechanical dictation (for example, God used the human writer as a musician uses his instrument). But such figures are not to be taken literally; elsewhere the same authors admit the free use of the sacred writers' faculties, although it is a fact that they did not insist on the human side of Scripture.

Quite apart from errors of either kind, there has been widespread confusion between revelation and inspiration. This point will be considered in the next section when the differences between the prophet and the inspired writer are examined.

3. REVELATION AND INSPIRATION

In his *Summa Theologiae*, St. Thomas has a treatise on prophecy (II-II, qq. 171-175). He deals there with the question of prophetical inspiration. He deliberately restricts his field of investigation, considering a prophet, in the strictest sense, as one who receives a revelation from God; consequently the divine influence is manifest to the maximum extent and there is little room for human initiative. The prophetic charism illuminates the prophet's judgment and guarantees the divine truth of the message he has received and is to communicate. What is involved is judgment of the speculative order: knowledge of truth in order to teach it faithfully. It should be noted carefully that, in this treatise, St. Thomas does not consider, not even indirectly, scriptural inspiration; hence his treatment cannot be applied to our subject. Nevertheless, the principles involved in his study of prophecy may be profitably invoked in the study of inspiration.

We would not be just to the mind of St. Thomas if we regarded a prophet as merely a docile and faithful instrument, whose words are an exact echo of the words of God; but here as elsewhere, St. Thomas has not been too happily served by his commentators.[1] What is undeniable is that, until modern times, the inspiration of the Bible was understood in the same way as the inspiration of a prophet—so-imagined. Patristic and medieval exegesis—in practice at least—ignored the human writer: the Bible was the word of God, and God spoke with the fullness of truth in the least word of Scripture. Even when the literal meaning of a passage seemed to exclude any spiritual message, allegorical exegesis readily discerned a deeper value beneath the letter. This uncomplicated conception, shared by Protestants and Catholics alike, remained more or less undisturbed until the nineteenth century. Modern studies, however, have made it clear that we may not ignore the human writer, for only through the words and ideas of the sacred writer can the divine message be discovered and understood.

Prophetic inspiration, in the strict sense described above, is quite rare in the Bible—if not altogether absent. We have to remember

---

[1]For an excellent study of the real dimension of St. Thomas' thought, see Victor White, *God and the Unconscious* (Cleveland, Ohio: Meridian, 1961), pp. 125-57.

that St. Thomas' approach, which is wider than the later presentation
of his thought would lead one to suppose, was influenced by the
culture he had inherited, that of Plato and of Aristotle. In this system
speculative knowledge holds first place; one reaches out to God by
reflection and contemplation. The Greeks regarded divine oracles
as the communication of superior truths to men, through the medium
of inspired poets or by prophetesses moved by the divinity. Sharing
this outlook, the patristic tradition tended to regard the inspired
writers as transmitters of "revelations" and the Bible as a collection
of truths proposed to men. Medieval theology saw the matter no
differently. For St. Thomas, too, the role of the prophet was primarily
intellectual: he received from God truths otherwise unknown, and
passed them on to men.

Today, however, we are keenly aware that the Semitic mentality,
which produced the Bible, stands in notable contrast to the Greek
mentality. Throughout the Bible the accent is not so much on knowledge and contemplation as on action and on love. This is true not
only of the Old Testament but also of the New in which the Word
made flesh is less interested in delivering to men the ultimate objects
of contemplation than in addressing to them the ultimate invitation
of love and in treading for them that path of renunciation and
thanksgiving, of trust and of obedience, which leads to the Father.
St. Thomas did not have (and could not have had, since it is the
result of modern scholarship) this understanding of the nature of
the Bible. This also we have to keep in mind when applying his
principles to the inspiration of the Bible. If we are to view the
matter clearly, we must grasp what the Bible itself means by "revelation" and "inspiration." In doing so we shall abstract from the very
precise technical sense these words have in scholastic theology.

1) Revelation in the Bible

We begin to understand the biblical idea of "revelation" when we
have grasped the meaning of the term *dabar* ("word"). This Hebrew
term is not only the representation of a concept, as is the Greek
logos, but also means "thing," or, more precisely, the background of
the thing, where its profound sense is to be discerned.

The word of Yahweh is an objective energy which "comes" (Jgs.
13:12,17), which is "fulfilled" (1 Kgs. 2:27). Sent by God into the

world as a supremely efficacious agent (Is. 55:11), it does not weaken or fail, but "stands forever" (40:8). It is creative (Gn. 1:1 ff.; Pss. 33 (32):9; 147 (146):15-18); it rules history (Is. 44:26-28) and carries out the vengeance of God (Is. 9:7; Wis. 18:15 f.).

This concrete, existential use of "word" points the way to the understanding of the correlative notion of "revelation." In the Bible, God does not ordinarily have recourse to visions nor does he speak by means of oracles repeated word for word by a prophet. The Bible is not a sum of abstract "truths," a body of doctrine. What Scripture reveals is God himself, a living Person: the Creator who governs the world (Is. 45:12); the Holy One who summons men to a service of love (Ex. 20:1 ff.; 34:6; Hos. 11:1 ff.); the Lord of history who guides times and events towards a goal of salvation (Ex. 14:18; Am. 2:9 f.; Jer. 32:20; Is. 45:1 ff.; 52:10). This God does speak to men, but he also reveals himself by the marvels of nature and the events of history. His "divine name, Yahweh [I am who I am], is not so much the manifestation of his essence as the invitation to recognize him—in his continuing and efficacious direction of the history of salvation—as the one and only true God who controls the destiny of Israel . . . (Hos. 12:10; 13:4; Is. 45:5)."[2] In short, God reveals himself by his impact on the life of individuals and on his whole people.

The distinctive biblical point of view is more evident still when we turn to the full revelation of the New Testament. Jesus revealed the Father's loving design—not a system to be grasped, but a way to be followed. His "truth" is not an object of intellectual speculation, it is "way" and "life" (Jn. 14:6). He spoke, but his person and his actions spoke louder than his words. He did not only speak the word, he is the substantial, living Word, the Word made flesh. His essential revelation was himself, and his message was to blaze the trail which he asks his followers to walk, the way that passes by death to life.

It is clear that, if we are to be true to the data of the Bible, we may not confine "revelation" to declarations of speculative truth; it must include the whole field of God's self-manifestation; it must

[2]Pierre Benoit, *Aspects of Biblical Inspiration*, trans. J. Murphy-O'Connor and S. K. Ashe (Chicago: The Priory Press, 1965), pp. 68-69. In this treatment of revelation and inspiration, I am entirely indebted to Father Benoit.

embrace actions as well as words, for God is no abstract essence but a living Person. And, "the interpreter of revelation will not be merely one who, having 'understood' a vision or an oracle, has transmitted to others its content. He will be a witness who has encountered God, or rather to whom God has made himself personally known in the mystery of his creative and salvific love."[3] The sacred writers have experienced, and have captured for us, this revelation; they have indeed written of nature and of history, for the guidance of the people of God.

To restrict revelation to "prophecy" strictly so-called would entail the risk of neglecting all the existential context of action, of history, and of personal intervention which surrounds the spoken word of God by a living and lived word. To fail to recognize revelation in the events of sacred history just as much as in the enlightenment granted to the prophets would mean a dangerous impoverishment of the extreme richness of that encounter which God offers to men in the Bible. "In many passages of the Bible, God does not teach men a new truth; rather, he shows them how to read the divine books of nature and of history with a supernaturally enlightened eye. Is not this, in brief, the principal goal of his revelation: to manifest himself as he who creates, guides, and saves?"[4]

2) *Inspiration in the Bible*

Apart from the *theopneustos* of 2 Tm. 3:16, the term "inspiration" does not appear in the Bible, although there is frequent reference to the action of the Spirit on men. Varied as the usage is, however, it is significant that never is the Spirit said to move a man to think or to write, but always urges to speak or to act. "There is in the Bible a real *inspiration to act*, that is, an efficacious movement of the Spirit of Yahweh seizing a man in order that he might perform certain actions."[5] Nor are these only sporadic exploits or symbolic actions; they are also enterprises of great moment and of decisive historical import. God sent his Spirit upon Moses to direct him in leading the Exodus, in founding the Covenant, and in governing the people (Is. 63:11,13). Moses' successor, Joshua, is "a man in whom is the Spirit" (Nm. 27:18). When David was anointed king

---

[3]*Ibid.*, p. 71.
[4]*Ibid.*, p. 77.
[5]*Ibid.*, p. 78.

of his people, "the Spirit of the Lord came mightily upon him from that day forward" (1 Sm. 16:13). Thus, the divine Spirit raises up and stimulates those whom God has charged with the conduct of sacred history.

Then, especially in the prophets, there is an *inspiration to speak* (Nm. 22:38; 2 Sm. 23:2; Is. 59:21; Ez. 11:5; Hos. 9:7; Lk. 1:15, 17,41,67; 2:27,36; 2 Pt. 1:21). The prophets are the interpreters of the Spirit. Their inspiration consists in hearing and pronouncing those "oracles of Yahweh" which teach and direct the people. But, we repeat, the Bible has no instance of the Spirit laying hold on a man in order to move him to think or to write.

Of course we may still speak of "scriptural" inspiration; but, in view of the evidence, we must be careful not to make of it the absolute and exclusive manifestation of inspiration in the Bible. We may legitimately speak of scriptural inspiration because the Bible is indeed the term, willed and directed by God, of the events of sacred history and of the oral teaching which it preserves in written form. Nevertheless we would be wise not to restrict inspiration to this ultimate stage, but to extend it, as the Bible does, to the earlier and no less important stages of the word lived by the pastors and leaders of the people of Israel.

When we say that the Bible never shows us the Spirit coming upon a man in order to move him to think, we do not mean that Scripture has no place for thought or knowledge. The fact, as we have seen, is that, in the Bible, "knowledge" is never speculative only: it is a matter of the heart and of action as much as of the intellect. Inspiration, in the Bible, is a movement of the Spirit which touches the whole man; it makes him know or think only by first urging him to act or speak or write. "To consider it exclusively from the point of view of speculative knowledge is to commit oneself to an operation which may well result in the death of the patient."[6]

We may conclude that, when seen in the perspective of the Bible, it does seem wrong to regard inspiration and revelation as two distinct charisms of knowledge, one concerning the judgment, the other referring to the presentation of truth. It is no less arbitrary to separate them chronologically, to say that inspiration begins where revelation ends. In fact, inspiration and revelation, in Scripture, are

---

[6]*Ibid.*, p. 83.

distinct, but they operate simultaneously. A man is raised up and moved by the Spirit to direct a phase of the history of salvation, to speak as a prophet, or to write down the essentials of this divine pedagogy; but all this activity is "revelation," the personal manifestation of a living God. God *reveals* the Truth which he himself *is* in terms of the lived, spoken, and written experiences of his people; and to that end he inspires leaders, preachers, and writers, who perceive this Truth and who pass it on to the people by living it, by speaking it, and by writing it.

SUMMARY

1. Revelation, in the Bible, is not the communication of abstract truths, but the concrete and living manifestation of a personal God as Creator and Savior. This manifestation may be made by the events of sacred history (*Heilsgeschichte*) and by the wonders of nature, as well as in the words of inspired prophets and writers.

2. The inspired writers are moved to understand and to transmit this divine revelation by action and by word quite as much as by writing; the inspiration which urges them is not only "scriptural," but also, and especially, "pastoral" and "prophetical." It is not only a charism of the intellectual order, but a wider impulse which moves a man in any sphere that can bring about a living encounter with God.

3. Inspiration and revelation are not identical, but neither do they conflict; nor does one follow the other in chronological order: they operate simultaneously and harmoniously. God reveals himself in nature, in history, and, ultimately, to and through the minds of men; in so doing, however, he elevates man and fills him with his Spirit in order that man may live, speak, and finally write the message of living Truth which flows from this encounter with God.

| *The Psychology of Inspiration*

DEFINITION OF INSPIRATION
PRACTICAL JUDGMENT AND SPECULATIVE JUDGMENT
REVELATION, INSPIRATION, AND JUDGMENT
HOW THE INSPIRED WRITER IS MOVED
THE EXTENT OF INSPIRATION

Although we have seen how wide and fluid are the biblical notions of revelation and inspiration, we must guard against forcing them into ready-made and tight-fitting categories. But we have seen, too, that it is legitimate to speak of *scriptural* inspiration, which implies not the uttering or the mechanical writing down of words received from on high, but the composition of a book, with all the initiative and human labor that such a task demands. In order to bring out more clearly the true nature of scriptural inspiration, we must turn to psychology.

1. DEFINITION OF INSPIRATION

When we wish to attempt an analysis of the psychology of inspiration we cannot take a better starting point than the familiar definition of inspiration, in terms of the divine influx and its effect on the human authors, given in *Providentissimus Deus*: "For, by supernatural power, he [God] so moved and impelled them to write, he so assisted them when writing, that the things which he commanded, and those only, they, first, rightly understood, then willed faithfully to write down, and finally expressed in apt words and with infallible truth; otherwise, it could not be said that he was the author of the entire Scripture."[1]

This definition is concerned with two acts: (1) the acceptance of truth by the sacred writer; (2) the communication of truth. Although

[1]Pope Leo XIII; see Denz. 1952.

these are acts of the intellect and will, we shall see that the role of judgment is paramount. However, all the faculties of the writer are touched by the charism of inspiration.

Most often, the sacred writer is not aware that he is being used and moved by God; hence he sets about his work in a perfectly natural way. He may feel the need or realize the opportuneness of putting forward some truth about God or about God's dealing with men; then he sees how, according to his ability and talent, the point may be most effectively made; finally he writes the book. All the while, although he did not know it, he was guided by the Holy Spirit. The divine influence which inspired him in the first place continued to move him until the book was written, for the purpose of scriptural inspiration is to produce an inspired book.

2. PRACTICAL JUDGMENT AND SPECULATIVE JUDGMENT

By no means the least important contribution to the study of inspiration is the distinction made between the role of the speculative judgment and the role of the practical judgment, and the realization of the preponderant part played by the latter in the case of an author.[2] The scholastic view gives the first place in scriptural inspiration to the speculative judgment, according the practical judgment the subordinate position of execution. The psychological reality is quite other. We can readily imagine a writer approaching his task in different ways. He may wish to write primarily in order to present a certain truth; thus he may produce a scientific treatise. In such circumstances his work will be dominated by his speculative judgment, and the practical judgment will be involved to a lesser extent; it will have its role to play, of course, because the writer will wish to present his thought as clearly as he can, but this part will be subordinate.

On the other hand, it can easily happen that the practical judgment may have the major role, because an author can put his ideas across in other ways than by tract. A novel, for instance, or a play— if these are to be worthy of the name—will have something to tell us; the talented writer does not lecture but clothes his message in

---

[2]The speculative judgment is concerned with the knowledge of truth and, in a writer, with truth to be communicated. The practical judgment is concerned with the means of communication.

art form. His speculative judgment does indeed bear on the truth that is the kernel of his work, but the practical judgment commands and regulates the whole operation. It is obvious that the two methods indicated are very different. The first is manifestly aimed at making a point clearly and with little thought for literary presentation; it is the direct approach, but it is not necessarily the more effective, for, how many are going to read a technical treatise? The other method is more subtle and has in mind a wider public; it seeks to win men over to a point of view instead of trying to convince them by logic. This, to an overwhelming extent, is the method of the biblical writers.

It follows that we should not expect to have dogmas hurled at us from every page of the Bible. The sacred writers have often sought to stir the hearts of their readers; they have consoled them or warned them or, quite simply, striven to win their interest. The New Testament writers are always concerned with Christ; the Old Testament writers have always wanted, ultimately, to teach men about Yahweh and his works, but they have done so in a variety of ways. In short, the biblical writers were moved to use their literary talents to the full in the presentation of their message; in reality, then, their practical judgment was dominant while they wrote. Indeed, far from always taking the primary place, speculative judgments inevitably will follow *after* the practical judgment of scriptural composition and under its influence.

In this important matter it is necessary to be precise. Therefore the following affirmations must be made:[3]

1. In the composition of an inspired book (as of any book), speculative judgments do not necessarily precede practical judgments, but may be concomitant or follow after. Many particular speculative judgments are formed as the work proceeds and according to the needs of the book.

2. These speculative judgments may be qualified by practical judgments. The statements, suggestions even, which a writer makes in the course of his work are marked by the direction given to his work, by its purpose, by his manner of expression—in short, by his literary form. All of this pertains to the sphere of his practical judg-

---

[3] See Pierre Benoit, *Aspects of Biblical Inspiration*, trans. J. Murphy-O'Connor and S. K. Ashe (Chicago: The Priory Press, 1965), pp. 104-9.

ment which keeps in view the concrete end that he pursues as a writer; thus the formulation of speculative judgments will be modified by his practical judgment.

3. REVELATION, INSPIRATION, AND JUDGMENT

Further light may be thrown on the roles of speculative and practical judgments by linking these judgments with revelation and inspiration, as we have described them in the previous chapter. It seems that we might attach the illumination of the speculative judgment to the charism of "revelation"—taken in a wide sense—and reserve the direction of the practical judgment to the charism of "inspiration."[4]

The charism of *revelation* governs the whole field of speculative knowledge touched by the sacred writer under the movement of the Holy Spirit. It can bear on representations supernaturally communicated by God (revelation *stricte dicta*) or—and this is the normal way—on representations naturally acquired and on judgments already naturally formed (revelation *late dicta*). The essential factor is that, in either case, the divine light will enable the writer to judge on a higher plane and will guarantee the truths that now take on a new, supernatural quality; when they are taught in the (logically) later stage of inspiration, they are presented with the guarantee of divine authority.

The charism of *inspiration* directs the whole practical activity of the communication of truths received or illuminated by revelation. It also enlightens judgments, practical judgments, which direct the concrete execution of the work in conformity with the end in view and the literary form adopted.

Clearly, then, inspiration comes after revelation more in the logical order than chronologically; in fact, they are closely interwoven. The leading ideas will come first, but "revelation" does not end at this stage. By stimulating the sacred writer to do his work well, the Holy Spirit will move him to weigh his ideas more carefully, to phrase his message more precisely, to penetrate more deeply the truth which he is to communicate. Whenever his study and reflection lead to fresh supernatural perceptions, it is necessary that fresh

---

[4] See *ibid.*, pp. 121-24.

divine light intervene, that is, that "revelation" will come into play, in close connection with inspiration.

To round off this section, we give the conclusion of the brilliant article to which this and the preceding chapter owe so much.

This conception of revelation and inspiration concords better with the data of Scripture. We have seen above that revelation in the Bible embraces much more than the privileged case of visions accorded to certain prophets—the case on which St. Thomas centered his investigation. It englobes the totality of the personal manifestation of God, Creator and Savior, which is effected just as much by history as by oracles, and the entirety of the promulgation of the Word which reverberates not only in the ears of certain prophets, but in the minds and hearts of all those whom God causes to reflect on his salvific activity. It would be a good thing to restore to the term "revelation" this breadth and intellectual dynamism, which is not really reflected in the *acceptio rerum* of the scholastics.

Inspiration, conceived as the impulse and orientation which commands the production of a work, corresponds more closely to what it is in the Bible itself: the surge of the Spirit taking possession of a man to make him act, speak, write, and thus to manifest and proclaim divine Truth. We continue to speak of *scriptural* inspiration in relation to that particular impulse of the Spirit which gives rise to the production of a book, but we define it in such a way as to manifest its homogeneity with the other forms of inspiration: the inspiration to act (Pastoral Inspiration), by which God creates sacred history; and the inspiration to speak (Prophetic or Apostolic Inspiration) by which he creates the living oral tradition that nourishes his people.

Coming at the term of this great movement of the Spirit, *Scriptural Inspiration* finds its true place. It is the final impulse which brings into being the Book in which is written for all time the result, the resumé, the quintessence of the long education during which God revealed himself to men, manifesting to them in various ways, by deeds as well as by words, that Love-Truth which is himself. In this perspective, inspiration once again becomes the dynamic impulse of the Spirit, and revelation the manifestation of the Word, these two divine forces which have their supreme fulfillment in the Incarnate Word, conceived, guided, and raised from the dead by the Holy Spirit.[5]

4. HOW THE INSPIRED WRITER IS MOVED

It remains to examine *how* the sacred writer is moved by God. St. Thomas pointed the way: "The principal author of Scripture is the Holy Spirit; . . . the human writer was an instrumental author."[6]

[5]*Ibid.*, pp. 126-27.
[6]*Quodlibetum*, VII, a. 14 ad 5.

At first sight it may not seem very helpful to state that the human writer is an *instrument* of God, yet, rightly understood, this is the most satisfactory explanation. Indeed, the explanation of inspiration according to the principles of St. Thomas, with an explicit reference to instrumental causality, is specially commended in *Divino Afflante Spiritu*:

> For if our age accumulates new problems and new difficulties it also supplies, by God's bounty, new aids and helps to exegesis. Especially noteworthy among these is the fact that Catholic theologians, following the teaching of the holy Fathers and especially of the Angelic and Common Doctor, have investigated and explained the nature and effects of divine inspiration better and more fully than was the custom in past centuries. Starting from the principle that the writer in composing the sacred book is the *organon*, or instrument, of the Holy Spirit, and a living and rational instrument, they rightly observe that, under the influence of the divine motion, he uses his own faculties and powers in such a way that, from the book which is the fruit of his labor, all may easily learn "the distinctive genius and the individual characteristics and features of each" author.[7]

Therefore, it is not superfluous to sketch the philosophical doctrine of instrumental causality.

1. The main characteristic of an instrumental cause—which marks it off from a principal cause—is that it does not act by its own power, but must be moved to act by the principal cause if it is to do the work for which it was designed. Nevertheless, principal and instrumental causes form one principle of action.

2. Although the instrument depends for its exercise on the principal cause, it has its own innate and proper potentiality which comes into play when it is moved.

3. But the principal cause does not only move the instrument; it also *elevates* it to produce an effect in an order higher than that of its own native power.

4. At the same time, the instrument modifies the action of the principal cause, since the latter must adapt itself to the nature and quality of the instrument.

5. From the intimate conjunction and cooperation of the principal cause and of the instrumental cause follows the effect which neither the principal cause nor the instrumental cause alone can produce.

---

[7](London: C.T.S.), n. 37.

The whole effect is attributed to the instrumental cause, even though the order of being of the effect is of the same order as that of the principal cause.

An example may help to make the reasoning easier to follow. When a man sits down to write a letter, he usually takes a pen in hand. The pen is designed for writing, but it will never write until it is moved to do so. Further, the pen, of itself, is capable of making signs on paper, no more than that. Moved and elevated by the writer, however, it makes intelligible signs, that is, words and sentences. Now it is not true to say—although it does seem true at first sight— that the pen makes the signs only while the writer alone is responsible for their intelligibility. In fact, the intelligible content cannot be divorced from the signs (a word must signify something, otherwise it is a meaningless scrawl), and these have been caused by the pen. The pen has been moved and elevated to produce an effect of a higher order and it is responsible for the whole of that effect: it has produced signs that have meaning.[8] A writer does not, of course, have to use a pen, he may wish to type—but then he *has* to use a typewriter; or, if he wishes to write an elegant hand, he must have a good pen. In other words, the action of the principal cause is always modified by the quality of the instrument.

Now we may apply the philosophical notion of instrumental causality to the phenomenon of scriptural inspiration. We shall do so by setting out another series of propositions.

1. Because the action of the instrument, precisely as an instrument, is identical with the action of the principal cause, God is the principal Author of Scripture.

2. Principal and instrumental causes form one principle of action as subordinating cause and subordinate cause. The whole effect is to be attributed to each at the same time: to the former as *moving*; to the latter as *moved*.[9] They are not coordinated causes, each of which produces a part of the effect. Thus God and the sacred writer

---

[8]The reason for insisting on this will be made clear in Chapter Six.

[9]The situation is not quite the same as in n. 5 above, p. 40. Here the principal cause is divine; therefore there is nothing in the effect which he has not caused. In the case of a human principal cause, this is not true. For instance, when I type, it is not I but the machine that forms the letters; I am not responsible for this more material side of the process. But the typewriter, moved by me, has produced the whole effect: material signs *with an intelligible content*.

are each the author of Scripture: God as the principal cause; the sacred writer as instrumental cause.

3. In the concourse of principal and instrumental causes, the effect produced is in the same order of being as that of the principal cause. Therefore Scripture is supernatural, and differs essentially from any other book.

4. But the whole book is to be attributed to the sacred writer. The human author, although moved by God as an instrument, acts in a truly human fashion. His natural faculties are in no way suspended or suppressed, but he exercises his own proper activity, as he does in writing any book.

5. The action of the principal cause is modified by the qualities of the instrument; any shortcomings in the effect are to be attributed to the defectiveness of the instrument. So, too, the distinctive character and style of the different writers are readily discernible in the Bible.

6. The sacred writer, as a man, is an instrument *sui generis*; he is an instrument of a special kind proper to his rational nature. God, as principal cause, moves the sacred writer according to his nature as man; God moves him through his intellect, will, and executive faculties.

The last point made is of particular importance here. The principle of instrumental causality may be validly invoked and applied, but we have to keep in mind one fundamental factor: all the instruments that we use are inanimate, but the instrument used by God in the production of Scripture is a *human* instrument, a man with intelligence and free will; God, in moving this unique instrument, fully respects his intelligence and his freedom. How this last can be is mysterious, but it is only one aspect of a more far-reaching mystery (and we must not forget that inspiration is, in the last analysis, a mystery). Our theology teaches us that God, by a motion of grace, can move man from within and move him infallibly, yet all the while preserving his character of a free being.[10] It is precisely in this sense that God uses the sacred writer as an instrument. Under the supremely efficacious impulse of the Holy Spirit the human author is infallibly moved to think and to write what God wills and

---

[10]See St. Thomas Aquinas, *Summa Theologiae*, I-II, q. 109, a. 6 ad 1; q. 111, a. 2 ad 2.

as God wills it. Carried along by this motion, the writer is an instrument, but the force which moves him, far from diminishing his natural powers, augments them instead. He is a very special instrument, in a manner proper to his nature as a rational being.

At the same time, however, God adapts his message to the intelligence and culture of his chosen instrument; that is to say, the sacred writer, like any instrument, modifies the action of the principal cause. While the *whole* Bible is to be attributed to God (who moved the writers) and to the human authors (as moved by God), nevertheless the special characteristics of the writers were not submerged, but are clearly visible in each book. Many of the writers chosen by God were highly talented, and they exploited their literary gifts to the full in presenting the divine message. Others who served God's purpose were not so gifted; hence some parts of Scripture are, from a literary standpoint, quite pedestrian. But, gifted or not, it is through these human instruments that God speaks to us from one end of the Bible to the other.

5. THE EXTENT OF INSPIRATION

If, as we have seen, the whole Bible is to be attributed to God, it follows logically—indeed necessarily—that all of it is inspired: verbal inspiration (that is, inspiration extending to the very words) must be admitted. Many have balked at this, and the Church has had to intervene more than once in order to prevent an undue restriction of the divine charism.[11] Yet it is understandable that the concept should prove an embarrassment, for, on the face of it, verbal inspiration does seem to be excessive. And it is indeed excessive if we conceive of inspiration as being exactly the same in every part of Scripture.

The truth is that inspiration is not a univocal concept, but an analogical concept. "Human nature," for instance, is a univocal concept because all men possess it in the same way. "Life," on the other hand, is an analogical concept, for it may be predicated of men, animals, and plants. We may speak of life, in a true sense, in each case, but it is clearly not the same in each case.[12] Similarly, all the

---

[11]See *Enchiridion Biblicum*, nn. 124, 202, 455, 499.

[12]See Paul Synave and Pierre Benoit, *La Prophétie* (Tournai: Desclée, 1947), pp. 328-38; English edition, *Prophecy and Inspiration,* trans. Avery R. Dulles and Thomas L. Sheridan (New York: Desclee, 1961), pp. 119-32.

parts of Scripture are truly inspired, but not all are inspired in quite the same way.

No part of Scripture falls outside the influence of inspiration. The least text of the Bible is part of an individual book (and part, too, of the ensemble which is the whole Bible) and it has its role to play in the complete work. When he adds a secondary fact here or a colorful detail there, the human author acts as a writer conscious of his art; he knows that these less important elements will help in the presentation of the special truth he wishes to convey or in the general effect he wishes to produce.

> Such a detail is really inspired, but in its place and according to its role—which may be quite secondary. While regarding it as apt, the human writer accorded it little importance and paid it little attention. Consequently, the Holy Spirit, whose sovereign action is so completely one with that of the writer, has not shed his light on this point, or guaranteed the truth of it, in the same way that he does in another matter infinitely more important. In the varied diffusion of the charism this detail has received but little light and little weight, and so we ought to take it if we do not wish to distort the true intentions of the human writer and, through him, those of God.[13]

We should recall that the biblical author is inspired to write a *book*; it would be ridiculous to argue that any one passage of a book is just as important as any other. Yet such a line of argument has raised Tobias' dog (to take a trite example) to the status of a major problem: Why should God have inspired the sacred writer to mention this animal together with the fact that it wagged its tail? In fact, the mention of the dog is no more than a homely touch introduced to enliven the story. The writer himself would certainly have regarded it as an insignificant detail; he chose it in view of the general effect (it was his practical judgment that was involved), since it is no more than a literary ornament. Nevertheless it is inspired, because the author was moved by God to write a book in which this detail, too, is a part. In short, many difficulties would vanish if it were clearly grasped, once and for all, that the Bible is inspired *literature*.

---

[13]Pierre Benoit, "L'Inspiration," *Initiation Biblique* (Tournai: Desclée, 1954), p. 25; English edition, *Guide to the Bible*, trans. E. P. Arbez and M. R. P. McGuire (New York: Desclee, 1960[2]), pp. 29 f.

Throughout this chapter, in speaking of the sacred writer as an individual, we have simplified the actual situation. This had to be done if the principles were to be established and clearly presented. Having established them, however, we must advert to the fact that, in many cases, the authorship of the sacred books is a complex matter; for many books have been retouched and developed over long periods, even over centuries.

> In short, the Bible appears to us more and more as a complex work on which successive generations have labored, as an edifice which many hands have helped to build. It is a collective work, the work of a whole people which has deposited in it, through the centuries, the treasure of its tradition. . . . This complex genesis of the sacred books changes nothing of their sacred character, for it is the final result, the Book in its last state, which the Church has received as canonical Scripture: it is this that is inspired. It is therefore necessary to admit that all those who contributed to produce it enjoyed inspiration. . . . But the influx of inspiration will not have been the same for all the laborers who have toiled at the work of God. He will have moved one to write the substance of the book, another to retouch it and make this or that addition.
>
> Clearly, the latter is not inspired in the same manner as the former; each shares in the charism to the extent, great or small, that he collaborates in the book. In the different authors, as in the different parts of the Book, as in the different faculties of the writer, we find that analogical distribution of the charism of inspiration which alone does full justice to the concrete reality of Scripture.[14]

In this context we should recall what has been written above of biblical inspiration—the outline of its variety and of its range. Those who guided the course of sacred history, no less than those who spoke the word of God, were moved by the Spirit. And although the biblical *writers* may have been moved in a special way in view of their precise contribution, we should not forget that the Bible is only the term, willed and directed by God, of every event of that saving history and of all the oral teaching which it preserves in written form. Inspiration extends to the earlier stages of the lived and spoken word.

---

[14]*Ibid.*, p. 26; English edition, pp. 30 f.

| FIVE | *The Inerrant Word* |

THE EXTENT OF INERRANCY
THE INTENTION OF THE SACRED WRITER
INERRANCY AND HISTORY
LITERARY FORMS

Because Sacred Scripture is divinely inspired, and hence has God for its Author, it follows that it is inerrant, that is to say, free from all error. Inerrancy is no more than a corollary—though a necessary corollary—of inspiration and, like inspiration, it has been misunderstood and misrepresented. This may be, to some extent, because the term is somewhat negative; it would be more rewarding to speak of the "truth" of Scripture, but "inerrancy" is undoubtedly the current expression. At any rate, most attacks on the Bible have been launched along this front; far too often the defenders have been lured or forced into positions that were precarious and even false.

1. THE EXTENT OF INERRANCY

Just because Scripture is everywhere inspired it does not follow that it is always and everywhere inerrant—in a positive sense. Inspiration and inerrancy are coextensive, but under either of two aspects: positively, when truth is at stake; negatively, in the forestalling of any teaching of error.[1] We have seen that *scriptural* inspiration governs the composition of a book, and much of what a writer says is, or at least can be, accessory to his leading ideas; and it is abundantly clear that the sacred writers are not, at all times and in every detail of their work, teaching something. Instead of "teaching" his

[1]See Pierre Benoit, "Inerrance Biblique," *Catholicisme* (Paris: Letouzey et Ané, 1963), V, 1546.

46

readers a writer may seek to touch their hearts, to stimulate, console, or please them. Even when his appeal is to their intellect, he can take steps to present his message in an accessible and agreeable manner. The sacred writers have not acted otherwise. Among the qualities of their work—beauty, charm, persuasiveness—truth stands high; by no means, however, is truth the only quality, nor is it always present.

We have remarked that, in an author, the practical judgment may play the leading part, whereas inerrancy touches the speculative judgment, in the measure in which that judgment is enlightened. Very often, however, one's approach to the Bible is colored by the idea of prophetical inspiration, causing one to feel that every sentence of Sacred Scripture is not only divinely inspired, but also divinely true. But the inspiration in question is scriptural inspiration, which does not imply that truth must be positively taught in every part of Scripture, although it does completely exclude the deliberate teaching of error.

We may get a better grasp of this if we see what is meant by "error." Error involves a deliberate *judgment* at variance with existing reality. Error is possible only when there is a definite intention to express a particular aspect of truth and when something is positively stated. For instance, when we describe the sun as rising we are not in error, because we limit ourselves to sensible perception, to what we can see; we do not go beyond this, we do not pass judgment on an astronomical theory. If, however, on the basis of the apparent movement of the sun, we were to affirm, as a scientific fact, that the sun really does move around the earth, that affirmation would be erroneous: a deliberate judgment at variance with reality.

This point has been made, with admirable clarity, by Dom Celestin Charlier:

> Two things are required for error: first a judgment, something formally affirmed and taught, and secondly an explicit intention to express that precise aspect of truth which is in fact not expressed. Where nothing is taught, but only an opinion given, or where a universally accepted idea is received without judgment being passed, then there is no error. Where a given affirmation is erroneous only from a point of view entirely foreign to the formal intention of the writer and the demands of the readers he is addressing, there is no real error. In fine, error is part of the philosophical definition of evil. Evil is the absence of a good which is *due*; error is the absence of the truth which *may be demanded*. Nobody can be accused of error, of failing to express

himself perfectly, if it is not his intention or his duty to his contemporaries to do so.[2]

2. THE INTENTION OF THE SACRED WRITER

In the last analysis it is a writer's intention that will determine the
truth or falsehood of whatever he writes. Normally, he will treat
of things and speak of them from one aspect only. The stars, for
example, are not seen in quite the same way, and obviously are
not described in the same way, by the astronomer who studies their
laws, by the poet who is moved by their beauty, and by the religious
thinker who recognizes in them a striking effect of the power of the
Creator. We cannot say that the two latter are in error when they
speak only according to their point of view. Now the biblical writers
are certainly religious thinkers, and very often they are poets as well,
but they are never scientists. If we look for scientific truth in the
Bible, we shall not find it, simply because it is not there. This is
why, for instance, the creation of the universe is described according
to the unscientific opinions of the age in which the story was formed
—and it must be judged in the light of these opinions. Happily, it
is no longer necessary to insist that the Bible is not a scientific manual,
and one that is always up-to-date. It has been some time since the
last nail was driven into the coffin of concordism.

It is also well to keep in mind that not everything an author
writes is a categorical statement. This obvious observation has important implications because, as the Biblical Commission tells us,
we must accept as asserted, enunciated, or suggested by the Holy
Spirit whatever the sacred writer asserts, enunciates, or suggests.[3]
This statement clearly allows for different degrees of affirmation.
Sane exegesis of any scriptural passage will determine, in each case,
just how far the sacred writer guarantees his ideas. The truth of
what he says will be involved to that extent and no more. He may
venture an opinion or he may even express hesitation or doubt. We
must respect these qualifications, because God, who speaks through
the sacred writer, has condescended to accept them.

---

[2]*The Christian Approach to the Bible* (Westminster, Md.: Newman, 1958), pp.
216 f.

[3]See *Enchiridion Biblicum*, n. 420.

We may go a step farther and say that a writer can affirm something which he does not put forward as a fact to be believed. We find the clearest example of this—because the matter is beyond question—in the parables. Our Lord (whose words are necessarily true quite apart from the fact that they are recorded in an inspired book) tells of the son who asked for and received his inheritance and then squandered it in a foreign country; and tells, too, of the reaction of the young man's father and brother to his homecoming. All this is affirmed, but none of our Lord's hearers and no reader of the Gospel believes that the story is true and that the characters are historical. The story is told in order to illustrate the loving mercy of God and to serve as a warning to some proud and critical Pharisees. The details of it aim at making this twofold point effectively: they serve no other purpose; by themselves they have no special significance. A sacred writer, therefore, may use fiction, because fiction can be a vehicle of truth, even of divine truth. The parables bear this fact out; indeed, fictional works also can be found in the Old Testament. Clearly such writings must be judged according to the intention of their authors and not according to any of our preconceived ideas.

3. INERRANCY AND HISTORY

The problem of the Bible and physical science is, we have remarked, no longer a vital one; it is now fully realized that these are two quite distinct fields. No contradiction is possible between the Bible, correctly interpreted, and the certain conclusions of the profane sciences. History, however, approaches much more closely to the nature of the biblical message, which is essentially historical. Hence, even though there is no reason why the divine charism should shed a light on the scientific analysis of the universe, there is every reason why it should bear on a history that witnesses to the unfolding of the saving plan of God. But here, too, there is room for caution.

In this scientific age we are plagued by a passion for material exactitude—a tendency which is very well illustrated in the field of history. Now, when we turn to the Old Testament we find that its historians were, by our standards, rather casual. They were little worried by exact chronology and they quite regularly omitted facts that did not suit their point of view or their purpose. They have given us a history that has glaring gaps and that is sometimes inaccurate. To our eyes this shortcoming is even less excusable, because they have often indicated that they had much more information at their disposal. Therefore, judged by our standards, they were at fault; but may we legitimately measure them by modern standards? We might turn the argument around and say that, for Old Testament writers, history in the modern style would be meaningless because it quite misses the one factor that can give it meaning.

The Old Testament historians had God always in mind and saw the hand of God in everything that happened. In the light of this truth, of this profound realization, details like exact chronology are seen in proper perspective. We pay lip service to the dogma of divine Providence, yet, in practice, we have lost sight of the constant activity of God in history. Does our more exact technique really compensate for the loss of that comforting vision? And when we turn to the New Testament we find not only the Providence of God, but God Incarnate—a God who not only acts in history but has become a fact of history.

We must remember that the biblical historian is not a modern historian; hence our modern criteria cannot be applied to the historical books of the Bible. The modern historian sees the historical fact, or tries to see it, in its objective reality, but this is not the only way of writing history.

> The religious historian, as we find him in the Bible, will consider the historical fact and report it only to the extent in which it can be inserted into the religious plan that is his real concern. The Holy Spirit who guides him will move him to speak of it only on this account, and will guarantee its truth only under the precise aspect which alone is the object of his teaching. It would be going against God's intention to turn his Scripture into a book of scientific history and to seek in it the truth proper to such a literary form. The charism of inspiration has lighted up the facts of history only from the angle that mattered to the purpose of the sacred Book, and it can very well have left all the rest in the background, in the shadow of imperfect and even inaccurate knowledge.[4]

But religious history is still history; it does not cease to be history just because it is not scientific. Those critics who so often have judged the Bible, the New Testament as well as the Old, to be

---

[4]Benoit, *op. cit.*, p. 37; English edition, p. 44.

unhistorical because it does not measure up to modern standards have been quite unscholarly in their method and have been guilty of a glaring anachronism. Scripture is a product of its own time and the scholarly approach will take full cognizance of the fact.

4. LITERARY FORMS

A happy result of the realization of the human aspect of the word of God, and of the fact that the sacred writers were children of their own time, is the further realization that their work must have been governed by the literary conventions of their epoch. The Bible is literature and it must be understood and interpreted as literature. Now, it is a common experience that terminology, especially when it is a foreign expression, can be very impressive and may seem to indicate a new and brilliant discovery. Thus some people speak of *genres littéraires* as if these were entirely novel, whereas the existence of different forms in literature is something we take for granted. Nevertheless it is true that, with regard to the Bible, precisely because its human aspect was not fully recognized, the application was very restricted. Now, at last, this situation has been rectified: it is admitted that Scripture does contain a variety of types.[5] At the same time it is fully realized that literary forms cannot be determined a priori; often we have to be well acquainted with the literary conventions of an age in which a writing took shape before we can establish its form. Clearly, too, the most fruitful field for the application of the principle is presented by the historical books.[6]

We have just remarked that we cannot legitimately measure the work of the biblical historians by our standards of historical exactitude. History in our sense is a modern science; hence it would be unrealistic to expect even the New Testament writers to have shared our twentieth-century preoccupations. But we must push our investigation of the historical books further. Should we, in fact, admit that some of these books were never meant to be historical? Today there can be little doubt that this is so; the realization that, in certain cases, we are not dealing with strict history or with history in any sense has disposed of a host of false problems. Some of the books

---

[5]*Divino Afflante Spiritu* has made this point clearly and with some emphasis; see the Catholic Truth Society translation, nn. 39-42.

[6]Although indeed it has to be seen whether all the books traditionally so described are really historical; and if so, in what sense and to what extent.

traditionally listed as historical have been so classified on the ground of appearances only. It would be well to remember that our division of the Old Testament writings into historical, prophetical, and didactic books betrays a Western mentality, and that the Jewish groupings of Torah, Prophets, and Writings is more satisfactory because more "biblical."

It is understandable, therefore, that there should have been such mistaken classification. We may still, for instance, if given no indication, readily take a well-written historical novel for a lively biography. If we are in doubt (and have no other means of knowing), we must depend on our knowledge of the technique of the novelist and the biographer and on our ability to check alleged historical facts against other facts of which we are sure. As a result it may transpire that a writing, which at first sight we had thought to be historical, is in reality not historical at all and was never meant to be historical. This is the exact position of Jonah, for example: it *appeared* to be a historical work and was uncritically accepted as such. The misunderstanding was aggravated by the quite unjustified prejudice that fiction was unworthy of God. Because of an amazing growth in our knowledge of the background to the Bible, we know better today (and Jonah is not an isolated case in the Old Testament). The recognition that fiction, or a fictional narrative built on a basis of historical facts, has its place in Scripture is of major importance. It means that our generation has a more enlightened approach to the Bible and is spared many false problems that plagued our predecessors.

Clearly the sacred writers may have employed any of the literary forms in use among their contemporaries "so long as they were in no way inconsistent with God's sanctity and truth."[7] Some have felt that this would exclude fiction—a singular conclusion in view of the parables. Few literary forms, past and present, could be excluded on this score; perhaps even then it would be by reason of the content rather than because of the form. It has been said that, whereas we can well imagine God inspiring a novelist like Dostoyevsky, we could never dream that he would inspire a pornographic

_____
[7]*Enchiridion Biblicum*, n. 559.

novel. This is true, but the observation is not altogether relevant, since in either case the form might be the same. We can hardly ever decide, in the abstract, what is becoming or unbecoming to God, for the divine condescension goes deeper than we know. When studying the word of God it is well to have in mind the stark reality of the Incarnation and the scandal of the Cross.

| SIX | *The Senses of Scripture* |

SECONDARY SENSES
FULLER SENSE AND TYPICAL SENSE
CONDITIONS AND CRITERIA OF THE SECONDARY
SENSES
THE SECONDARY SENSES AND INSPIRATION
A NOTE ON THEOLOGICAL CONCLUSION AND
ACCOMMODATION

From what we have seen of inspiration, it follows that, if we are to understand the Bible, we must look first for the meaning which the human writer intended, because this is what the Holy Spirit, as Author of Scripture, proposes to us first and foremost. To look for the meaning of the sacred writer is no more than common-sense, but to look for it *in the first place* points to a quality of the Bible that is unique: it implies that there is another meaning *which the human author has not intended.* In the course of this chapter we shall see that such secondary meanings exist, lying beneath the surface of the text.[1]

When we speak of the senses of Scripture, we refer to a meaning or meanings that really exist in a biblical text. To be quite clear, we should make an elementary distinction between "signification" and "sense." *Signification* is the notion which a word expresses in the abstract, independently of the speaker or writer or of any particular context. It is frequently multiple (for example, the Greek term *pneuma* = "wind," "soul," "spirit," "Holy Spirit"). *Sense* is the notion which a word expresses in the concrete, according to the intention of a speaker or writer and in a definite context.

---

[1]The matter of secondary senses, or more accurately, of a "fuller sense" (*sensus plenior*) in Scripture is, as a rule, discussed among Catholic scholars only. Not all of them would admit the existence of a fuller sense; and some of those who acknowledge such a sense would not explain it in quite the same way we do in these pages. The book and articles listed in our bibliography provide a thorough coverage of the whole question.

Normally when we speak of sense we mean the *literal* sense, that is, the sense which the words immediately signify in the writer's intention. The literal sense may be either *proper* or *improper*, according as the words are taken in their direct or their figurative meaning. The division is clear, but the terminology is unfortunate.[2] For our purpose, we shall henceforth describe the literal sense as the *primary literal sense*; this leaves room for a treatment of the *secondary* senses that are also found in the letter of a biblical text, although they were not perceived by its human author.

1. SECONDARY SENSES

The primary sense of the Bible is that which follows immediately from the letter of the text as the human author understood it. It is found in every part of Scripture; otherwise we would have nonsense. But the Bible is no ordinary book. We have seen that the sacred writer is the instrument of the Holy Spirit and that, although his liberty has been respected, he still remains, in relation to God, a limited and defective instrument; thus, in certain cases, he may not have grasped the full import of the message which the divine Author wishes to express. The Holy Spirit, who has condescended to make use of a man in order to communicate with men, has not thereby confined himself irrevocably within human limitations. But he does not, in any way, infringe the liberty he has agreed to respect; nor does he trespass when he "reserves the right to go beyond his interpreter *in the same direction as his thought is tending,* and to enrich his words by broadening their meaning and adding new overtones which, far from confining or contradicting this thought, will actually deepen and extend it. Thus the primary meaning of Scripture may be supplemented by secondary meanings which prolong and amplify it."[3]

The fact of secondary senses stems from the very nature of the Bible and, more precisely, from the relationship between divine Author and human authors. The former is the Author of the whole Bible while each sacred writer is responsible for no more than a

---

[2] Besides the literal sense we find a *typical* sense in Scripture; this will be treated later in the chapter.

[3] Paul Synave and Pierre Benoit, *La Prophétie* (Tournai: Desclée, 1947), p. 357; English edition, *Prophecy and Inspiration*, trans. Avery R. Dulles and Thomas L. Sheridan (New York: Desclee, 1961), p. 150.

restricted portion of it. Moreover, God embraces the whole course of sacred history and of revelation, while the human writer is only one link in a chain. The divine Author outstrips the human author in three ways:[4]

1. The human writer speaks in one book only and then for a determined age and milieu; the divine Author speaks in all the books, from one end of the Old Testament to the other and from the Old Testament to the New. *Genesis, Isaiah,* and *Mark* are just so many distinct works when one thinks of the men who wrote them; but when one thinks of the God who inspired them, then they are seen to be so many chapters of the same great Book which he has directed from beginning to end.

2. It follows that the same God, although he has spoken throughout the centuries under different pens, has maintained enriching relationships between the succeeding stages of his unfolding Word. Under his guidance, words written by some have been taken up by other, later writers and now have fresh resonances not perceived by their first authors, although foreseen and prepared by him.

3. The God who inspires the written revelation guides also the sacred history which it mirrors. He is master of events as well as of minds, and he can have raised up persons or events or things which have the value of signs.

> He can speak a creative, concrete, existential language in which beings and events speak more eloquently than do the abstract terms of ordinary speech, a language of which God alone is capable and which he has used in a revelation that was lived and spoken before being set down in a book. It is a language which could not have been fully understood by its first interpreters, because the real portent of it can be grasped only at the close of the final act of the drama, when the roles of the various actors are at last clearly revealed in the light of the dénouement.[5]

2. FULLER SENSE AND TYPICAL SENSE

In view of the circumstances we have described, we may say that, in the Bible, beyond the primary literal sense, there is present—to an extent not easily determined—a deeper literal sense, contained in the letter, but foreseen and intended clearly and directly only by God.

---

[4]See Pierre Benoit, "La Plénitude de Sens des Livres Saints," *Revue Biblique,* 67 (1960), 162 f. For the remainder of this chapter, we will lean exclusively on a typically illuminating article of Father Benoit.

[5]*Loc. cit.*

We may speak, therefore, of a *fuller sense*: that fuller and deeper significance of a text which is intended by the divine Author and which is discovered in the light of further revelation, particularly in the light of the New Testament. The fuller sense, which is no more than a deeper insight into the primary literal sense, can be readily seen in the messianic prophecies of the Old Testament; they are clear to us because the Messiah has come, but the full meaning that we now perceive was intended by God from the first. Ultimately, the discernment of the fuller sense depends on the quality of the light in which one views a text. It is something like the process of infrared photography. Some of the Dead Sea Scroll fragments, for instance, are illegible to the naked eye, but the infrared camera reveals letters and words that were hidden. Nothing is added to the fragments, but the special light has brought to view something that was there all the time. So, too, the development of revelation reveals the hidden depths of earlier texts.

While the fuller sense is concerned with words (it is a deeper insight into the primary literal sense), the *typical sense* arises when the persons or events or things designated in the primary sense typify persons and events and things of a higher order and when this signification is intended by God. For example, we know from the New Testament that Melchizedek is a type of Christ the Priest, that the crossing of the Red Sea is a type of baptism, and that the brazen serpent raised up by Moses is a type of Christ on the Cross.[6] The typical sense is not a literal sense, because it is concerned with things and not with words. Nevertheless it is firmly based on the primary literal sense, for the significant facts or "types," which are the object of the typical sense, find their place in the Bible and are known to us only by means of the words; even though the human writer is unaware that he is describing a type, the type does emerge from his words. Abraham sacrificing his son and the manna feeding the people in the desert are types of Calvary and the Eucharist only insofar as these facts are recorded by the sacred writer and under the form in which he has recorded them. A biblical type is founded not only on a historical reality, but also on a literary existence. The latter may be the more important; for example, Melchizedek is a

---

[6]Melchizedek (Gn. 14:17-20; Ps. 110 [109]:4; Heb. 7:1-3); crossing of the Red Sea (Ex. 14:22, 29-31; 1 Cor. 10:1 f.); brazen serpent (Nm. 21:8 f.; Jn. 4: 14 f.).

type of the heavenly Priest (Heb. 7:3), not because he had no parents, but because Scripture has not stated that he had. It may even happen that the literary existence is the only real one (for example, Jonah is a literary, not a historical, figure). But the essential factor is that the typical sense, precisely because it is a *scriptural* sense, must be sought and found in the words of Scripture.

While there may be a close connection between fuller sense and typical sense, these remain distinct. What is specific in the typical sense is the correspondence, willed by God and expressed in his Scripture, of two concrete realities, each of which, although they have a common meeting point, is marked off from the other: manna and Eucharist; Noah's ark and baptism; the brazen serpent and Jesus on the Cross—the type and its antitype. The link factor in each case is a common religious value which sustains the correspondence (for instance, the divine gift of manna which nourished the Chosen People and the spiritual food of the Eucharist which feeds the new people of God). "It is on this continuous plane of religious values that the fuller sense is situated, while it is between the two planes of existence, the old and the new, that the typical sense comes into play."[7] The fuller sense follows on and accompanies the typical sense, but it is not identical with it.

The fuller sense may exist independently of a particular type, but it always has its roots in a general typology. Although the fuller sense does imply the homogeneous maturing of an idea, and not, immediately, the appearance of a new person or event, the growth of ideas that we have in mind could not occur without the emergence of something quite new on the plane of history. This new event is the fact of Christ: he has made all things new; it is in the sphere of this re-creation that the religious values of the Old Law find their accomplishment. In short, the whole of the old economy may be considered as one single, complex Type, whose component parts are particular types: not only persons and facts, but institutions like the Law, the Temple, the Kingship. Over against this, God has raised the antitype of the new economy, with its personages, its facts, and its institutions—the whole of it centered in Christ who gives to the old economy its decisive fulfillment. For, with Christ, all has, in

---

[7]Benoit, *art. cit.*, 178.

principle, been given; God has nothing more to add to this definitive word.

The fact of Christ constitutes a decisive leap forward, a radically new departure, a passage to a new plane which continues along the line of the old only after a vertical change of levels. We are not now on a higher step with other steps yet to climb; we have passed into a definitive order, into another world. In face of this decisive stage in which God has "made all things new" (Ap. 21:5), all the former stages represent only one and the same level of history, that of the old things.[8]

For this reason, the fuller sense and the typical sense are not found within the Old Testament taken by itself, or within the New Testament, but only within the Old Testament in the light of the New.[9]

3. CONDITIONS AND CRITERIA OF THE SECONDARY SENSES

The conditions required for a secondary sense, typical or fuller, and therefore also for its criteria, are *homogeneity* and *reproduction* (*reprise*).[10]

First, it is necessary that the secondary sense and the primary sense be *homogeneous*, that is, that the former should be a prolongation of the other in the same direction. The fuller sense, which is indeed a literal sense—although a secondary one—is substantially identical with the primary literal sense.

It adds to the latter a plus-value, but one that was already included in the objective meaning of the notion in question, although it had escaped the subjective perception of the author. . . . If, from the point of view of human psychology, we must distinguish between the primary sense and the secondary sense, from the point of view of God and of his Scripture we can say that these are one and the same literal sense.[11]

At first sight it would appear that this homogeneity does not apply to the typical sense, for we cannot overlook the vast distance and

---

[8]*Ibid.*, p. 185.

[9]The idea and acceptability of such a sense is by no means universal among biblical scholars. For a review of the varied opinions, see R. E. Brown, "The *Sensus Plenior* in the Last Ten Years," *Catholic Biblical Quarterly*, 23 (1963), 262-85.

[10]See *ibid.*, pp. 189-92.

[11]*Ibid.*, p. 190.

the diversity between type and antitype, between the brazen serpent and Christ on the Cross, for instance. Yet they do meet in the religious significance with which both are clothed in the message of revelation, a significance that is brought out in the words which sketch them. Thus the brazen serpent and Christ are both "raised up" and both bring "salvation" to those who gaze upon them in faith. Always there is a real, although mysterious, connection established by God, which is expressed by the fuller sense on the level of the text and by the typical sense on the plane of history.

The second condition and criterion is *reproduction* (*reprise*). The divine Author alone is capable of preparations in history and in the text of his Scripture, which he then brings to fulfillment on a higher level. But if we are to be sure that he has done so, he himself must let us know, for this is an element of the mystery of salvation whose secrets are his alone. God must point out to us that a particular situation of the New Economy had its authentic preparation willed by him, in a particular situation of the Old. It is in the New Testament that God has manifested his fulfillments; there he has commented on his own Word. This is done by "reproduction," by reproducing the figures and words of the preparation in the new context of fulfillment. Thus, for instance, the manna is the "bread from heaven" (Ps. 78 [77]:24, 105 [104]:40) and the Eucharist is the "true bread from heaven" (Jn. 6:32); the brazen serpent was "raised up" on a pole that the man "who sees it shall live" (Nm. 21:8), and the Son of Man "must be lifted up that whoever believes in him may have eternal life" (Jn. 3:14 f.). At the making of the Sinai Covenant, Moses poured out the blood of the victim upon the people, saying: "Behold the blood of the covenant" (Ex. 24:8); and Jesus said: "This is my blood of the covenant, which is poured out for many" (Mt. 26:28).

In all similar reproductions of the word of God there is a fuller sense. Indeed, much of the vocabulary in which the New Testament authors have expressed the mystery of Christ has been taken from the Old Testament. God guided them in this, just as he had guided the choice of words of their distant predecessors. Hence it is God who has brought about the homogeneous development of biblical language, in this way powerfully underlining the harmony of the two testaments.

4. THE SECONDARY SENSES AND INSPIRATION

We close this outline by raising the question of the inspiration of the *secondary* senses. While the fuller sense and the typical sense are not identical they do agree in this, that both are foreseen by God only and intended by him alone, while the sacred writer is not aware of them. According to the doctrine of instrumental causality, however, the *whole* Bible must be attributed to the human author; do these senses contradict the doctrine or can they be said to constitute an exception? It would appear, at any rate, that we cannot truly attribute them to the sacred writer.

It was in view of this objection that we stressed above[12] the fact that the intelligibility of a writing can and must be attributed to the writer's pen, because it, although an inanimate object, has produced intelligible writing. Now, both the typical sense and the fuller sense are contained in the text of Scripture—both must be based on a literal sense and that literal sense really contains the others. When, for example, the Old Testament author wrote of Moses raising up the brazen serpent, admittedly he wrote of that historical fact only: he had no idea that the serpent was a type of Christ raised on the Cross. Yet the typology is really contained in his words, even though he was not aware of it. The words are his, and the fuller meaning, foreseen and intended by God, is in those words. What we must admit is that, in these circumstances, the human writer is an instrument in the normal, stricter acceptation (and no longer in the very special manner of a rational instrument), for he is no more aware of those senses than the pen is aware of what it writes.

The action of God is not bounded by the consciousness of the sacred writer. Although God usually condescends to limit his message to the grasp of the writer, he is never tied to that manner of acting. The exception he makes—a relatively rare occurrence—is due to the nature of the Bible. He is the author of the whole of it, whereas each of the human authors has had a hand in part of it only. The typical and fuller senses spring from the unity of the Bible, a unity that cannot be grasped by men until the whole work is complete. The Old Testament writers could not have been aware of the fuller

---

[12] P. 41.

meaning of certain passages they had been inspired to write, but the whole meaning was there all the time, in their words. The doctrine of instrumental causality stands: the whole effect of inspiration must be attributed to God, as moving, and to the human writers as moved by God.

5. A NOTE ON THEOLOGICAL CONCLUSION AND ACCOMMODATION

A *theological conclusion* is a new application derived from a biblical text by way of a logical deduction which employs a minor premise drawn from reason. This is sometimes described as the "consequent sense," a misleading designation because it is not a scriptural sense; it is a deduction from Scripture.

Accommodation is the adaptation, based on some more or less close similarity, of the words of Scripture to some new situation or doctrine. The designation "accommodated sense" is to be deprecated, for accommodation is in no way a scriptural sense. Moreover, it must be used with great caution.[13]

---

[13]See *Divino Afflante Spiritu* (London: C.T.S.), nn. 32-33.

SEVEN

The Canon of Scripture

CANON AND CANONICITY

DEUTEROCANONICAL AND APOCRYPHAL BOOKS

THE FORMATION OF THE CANON

THE CRITERION OF CANONICITY

APPENDIX: THE QUMRAN SCROLLS

At the beginning of this study we listed the books of the Bible, now we have to examine the reason, or reasons, why we have accepted these books, and these only, as making up the body of inspired Scripture. We have to understand, too, why they are authoritative.

1. CANON AND CANONICITY

The Greek term *kanōn* meant originally a "measuring rod" and then, in a derived sense, a "rule" or "norm." The Fathers used the word "canon" for the "rule of faith," and the canon of Scripture was regarded as the written rule of faith. The idea which eventually prevailed was that of a determined collection of writings constituting a rule of faith. Ultimately the canon of Scripture came to mean what we understand by it today: the collection of divinely-inspired books received by the Church and recognized by her as the infallible rule of faith and morals in virtue of their divine origin. We may note that the designation "canonical," applied to Scripture, may be taken in an active or passive sense: (1) active—the Bible as the rule of faith and morals; (2) passive—the Bible as officially received by the Church.

Canonicity means that an inspired book, destined for the Church, has been received as such by her. Although all the canonical books are inspired, and no inspired book exists outside the canon, nevertheless the notions of canonicity and inspiration are not the same.

63

The books are inspired because God is their author; they are canonical because the Church has recognized them and acknowledged them to be inspired. For, the Church alone, by means of revelation, can recognize the supernatural fact of inspiration. Recognition by the Church adds nothing to the inspiration of a book, but it does clothe the book with absolute authority from the point of view of faith, and at the same time it is the sign and guarantee of inspiration.

2. DEUTEROCANONICAL AND APOCRYPHAL BOOKS

When we compare Catholic and Protestant versions of the Old Testament, we find that the latter lists 39 books—as does the Hebrew Bible—whereas Catholics accept 45 books.[1] This discrepancy, obviously a major problem in its own right, has also given rise to a confusing terminology. The disputed books are the following: Tobit; Judith; Wisdom; Sirach; Baruch; 1,2 Maccabees; together with parts of Esther and Daniel (that is, Est. 10:4—16:24; Dn. 3:24-90; 13-14). Catholics call these the *deuterocanonical* books—an unfortunate designation since it seems to imply that they are not of the same authority as the other books. What is really meant is that there was a certain hesitation about having them universally accepted as canonical, that is, as Scripture. By contrast, the *protocanonical* books are those whose claims have never been doubted in the Church. The deuterocanonical books of the Old Testament, together with 3,4 Esdras and the Prayer of Manasseh, are called the *Apocrypha* by Protestants, that is, "books which are not held equal to the sacred Scriptures, and nevertheless are useful and good to read" (Luther). Certain books of the New Testament (that is, Hebrews; James; 2 Peter; 2,3 John; Jude; Apocalypse) which, in the early Christian centuries, raised doubts or hesitancy in some quarters, are also called deuterocanonical; but these are now accepted by all Christians.

The name *Apocrypha* is applied by Catholics to certain Jewish and Christian writings which made some pretension to divine authority, but which, in fact, are not inspired Scripture. The Old Testament Apocrypha, the products of Judaism, are attributed to various patriarchs and prophets and reflect the religious and moral ideas of the

---

[1]This makes a difference of six books, whereas we go on to list seven. The explanation is that Lamentations, appended to Jeremiah in Catholic editions, is a separate book in Hebrew and Protestant Bibles.

Jewish world from the second century B.C. to the first century A.D. The New Testament Apocrypha are works of Christian origin. Attributed for the most part to apostles, they reflect the beliefs, doctrines, and traditions of certain circles, both orthodox and heretical, in the first centuries of the Church.

The confusion, mentioned above, is apparent: the term Apocrypha has one meaning for Catholics and an entirely different meaning for Protestants. The Apocrypha in the Catholic sense are designated *Pseudepigrapha* by Protestants.

3. THE FORMATION OF THE CANON

The one entirely sufficient criterion of the fact of inspiration is the testimony of the Church; and the Church, in the Council of Trent, formally defined the extent of the canon.[2] Although the question, as a dogmatic issue, is thereby settled for Roman Catholics, the following sketch of the formation of the canon of both Testaments is of real historical interest.

1) *History of the Canon of the Old Testament*

In the first century A.D. the Jews possessed a collection of sacred books which they held to be inspired by God and in which they saw the expression of the divine will, a rule of faith and morals. The witness of Josephus (*Contra Apionem* 1:8), of 4 Esd. (14:37-48), and of the Talmud is decisive. These books, distributed among the three divisions of Law, Prophets, and Writings, include all our protocanonical books. The New Testament is also a valuable witness because it contains quotations or allusions from most of these books; its silence in regard to the others is not significant, since there is no reason why all the Old Testament books should have been quoted. The threefold division is indicated: "Moses and the Prophets" (Lk. 24:27); "Moses, the Prophets, and the psalms" (Lk. 24:44).

The traditional division into Law, Prophets, and Writings—in that order—would seem to indicate, too, the chronological acceptance of each group of books. The *Pentateuch* took final shape in the fifth century, and from the time of Ezra the Jews accepted and officially recognized the collection of the Mosaic books as a sacred code.

---

[2]"Si quis autem libros integros cum omnibus suis partibus, prout in Ecclesia catholica legi consueverunt et in vetera vulgata latina editione habentur, pro sacris et canonicis non susceperit: *anathema sit*" (*Enchiridion Biblicum,* n. 42). The decree of Trent was endorsed in the First Vatican Council (see *ibid.,* n. 62).

The majority of the books that make up the second division (the "Former Prophets": Jos.-Kgs.; and the "Latter Prophets": Is.; Jer.; Ezek. and the twelve minor prophets) would have been accepted at about the same time. However, the collection cannot have been finally closed until sometime after the last of the prophets (the author of Zeph. 9-14), sometime in the late fourth century. Sirach (46:1—49:10) testifies that the list was complete before 180. We may safely conclude that the collection of Prophets was fixed in the first half of the second century, and from that time took its place side-by-side with the Law of Moses. The third group is composite and seems to have grown up around the collection of Psalms. Five books, the *Megilloth* (rolls)—Ct.; Ru.; Lam.; Qoh.; Est.—were read in the liturgy of the great feasts. The Chronicler's work (Chr.-Ez.-Neh.) comes last in the list. The group took shape between the fourth century and the end of the second century (cf. 1 Mc. 1:59 f.; 2 Mc. 3:14).

It should be noted that none of the three collections was established by an official decision, that is, placed among the books that had, in practice, been accepted. It is not surprising, then, to find differences in outlook. The position that we have considered, one which limited the canon to older and traditional books, is that of Pharisaism. We know that the Sadducees regarded only the *Pentateuch* as canonical. On the other hand, in Alexandria and in Qumran it was felt that God had not yet spoken his last word and that an inspired message might still be accepted. Thus, in the Diaspora,[3] our deuterocanonical books were accorded a real authority and it seems that the community at Qumran had attributed a similar authority to certain of their sectarian writings.

At the time of Christ there was still some uncertainty about the canon and the canonicity of certain books. It is not until after the destruction of Jerusalem (70 A.D.) that a group of Jewish doctors, seeking to preserve what remained of the past, met at Jamnia (= Yavne, 30 miles west of Jerusalem) about 90 A.D. and formally accepted the strict Pharisaic canon. On various grounds, including the fact that the Greek Bible had been adopted by Christians, certain of the books that formed part of that Bible (in effect, our deuterocanonical books) were rejected. The ruling of the Synod of

---

[3]The Diaspora ("dispersion") was the ensemble of Jews who lived outside Palestine, "dispersed" throughout the civilized world.

Jamnia was a decision for Jews only—and they henceforth accepted the shorter list. It could not be of universal import because the Church had now replaced the synagogue. At the time of the Reformation, the Protestants, wishing to make translations directly from the Hebrew, became keenly aware of this discrepancy; they ended by regarding the Jewish canon as the authentic one.

The Christian Church developed in the milieu of the Diaspora. In practice, the Bible of the Church was the Greek Bible; hence we find that citations in the New Testament are regularly from the LXX (Septuagint)—and these include explicit citations from at least three of the deuterocanonical books: Sir.; 2 Mc.; Wis. Most of the apostolic Fathers accepted the Old Testament as they found it in the LXX, or in the Old Latin versions based on the Greek. In the East, however, the differences between the books accepted in Palestine and Alexandria was kept in mind; this was an important factor in the controversy with Palestinian Jews. Hence Justin (second century), arguing with Trypho; Melito, bishop of Sardis (second century), in a list of accepted books; and Origen (third century) followed the Palestinian canon, as did Eusebius, Athanasius, Cyril of Jerusalem, Epiphanius, and Gregory Nazianzen (fourth century). So too did some of the Latin Fathers who were influenced by the Greeks, notably Rufinus and Jerome (fifth century).

The sixtieth canon of the Council of Laodicea (c. 360) supports the impression that the attitude of the East was, on the whole, unfavorable to the deuterocanonical books; for the Old Testament, it lists the books of the Hebrew Bible only. It is to be noted, however, that the Fathers admitted that these books could be read for the edification of the faithful and were useful for the instruction of catechumens. Besides, they often expressed great esteem for the books, admitting them for liturgical worship side-by-side with the others, and even cited them with the formulas: "It is written"; "God says in Scripture."

The attitude of the Eastern Fathers (together with Rufinus and Jerome) can be explained by two principal factors: 1) In controversy with the Jews, in order to have a common ground of argument, the Fathers confined themselves to the accepted Jewish canon. 2) Jewish apocrypha, making claims to canonicity, were in circulation; thus all books had to be carefully scrutinized, and the credentials of the deuterocanonical books did not seem to be quite as convincing as those of the others.

In the Western Church, however, no distinction was made between protocanonical and deuterocanonical books. Through the influence of St. Augustine, in reaction to St. Jerome and the Eastern attitude, the Councils of Hippo (393) and of Carthage (397 and 419) declared the disputed books to be canonical; Pope Innocent I did the same in a letter to Exsuperius of Toulouse (405). Therefore the complete canon as it was to be defined in the Council of Trent may be dated from St. Augustine. The Greeks later came around to the Western view, and at the Council "in Trullo" (692) accepted the entire canon.

2) History of the Canon of the New Testament

The Christian Church possessed, from the first day of its existence, a canon of inspired Scripture: the Old Testament. But for the early Church this Old Testament was, in its deepest sense, a prophecy of Christ—an acknowledgement that even here the ultimate authority was Christ himself. Christ had commissioned his Apostles to preach the Good News and to build up the Christian community, and had filled them with the power of the Holy Spirit. They had been eyewitnesses of his work and hearers of his words; and their importance was still greater in postapostolic times. Therefore the early Church had three authorities: the Old Testament; the Lord; and the Apostles. But the ultimate, decisive authority was Christ the Lord, who spoke immediately in his words and works and mediately in the testimony of his witnesses.

In the beginning the words of the Lord and the account of his deeds were repeated and related by word of mouth, but soon they began to be written down. In their missionary work, the Apostles found it necessary to write to certain communities. Some, at least, of these writings were exchanged among the churches and soon gained the same authority as the writings of the Old Testament. It is understandable, however, that some time elapsed before the collection of these writings from the time of the Apostles had taken its place with unquestioned authority beside the books of the Old Testament, especially when it is taken into account that many were occasional writings addressed to individual churches.

The written words of the Lord, the Gospels, although they are not the earliest New Testament writings, were the first set on a par with the Old Testament and recognized as canonical. About 140, Papias, bishop of Hierapolis in Phrygia, knows Mark and Matthew. Justin (c. 150) cites the Gospels as an authority. Hegesippus (c. 180) speaks of the "Law and the Prophets and the Lord." The martyrs of Scili in Numidia (180) have as sacred writings "the books, and the epistles of Paul, a just man"; only the Old Testament and the Gospels were called "Books," that is, Scripture. The writings of the apostolic Fathers furnish certain proof that, from the first decades of the second century, the great churches possessed a book, or a group of books, which was commonly known as "Gospel" and to which reference was made as to a document that was authoritative and universally known.

It is likely that already towards the end of the first century, or in the beginning of the second century, thirteen Pauline epistles (excluding Heb.) were known in Greece, Asia Minor, and Italy. All the manuscripts and text-forms of the Pauline epistles spring from one collection that agrees with our *Corpus Paulinum*. True, early collections show variations in the order of the epistles, but the number of writings remained the same. There is no quotation from Paul that is not taken from one of the canonical epistles, even though it is certain that the Apostle wrote other letters. Thus, about the year 125, there were two groups of writings which enjoyed the apostolic guarantee and whose authority was acknowledged by all the communities that possessed them. But there was no official pronouncement, and the collections varied from church to church.

We have little account of other apostolic writings in the first half of the second century. Clement knew Heb.; Polycarp knew 1 Pt. and 1 Jn.; Papias knew 1 Pt., 1 Jn., and Ap. In the second half of the century, Acts, Ap., and at least 1 Jn. and 1 Pt. were regarded as canonical; they took their place beside the Gospels and the Pauline epistles. We may note four factors which influenced the formation of the New Testament canon: (1) the many apocrypha which the Church rejected; (2) the heresy of Marcion who had set up his own canon, which consisted of an expurgated Lk. and ten epistles of Paul (excluding the pastorals and Heb.); (3) the Montanist heretics, who claimed further revelations from the Holy Spirit; (4) the great abundance of Gnostic writings.

It is generally admitted that, at the beginning of the third century, the New Testament canon comprised most, if not all, of the canonical books. The earliest list we have is that of the Muratorian fragment, a document discovered in the Ambrosian Library, Milan, in 1740; it gives the books which were accepted in Rome about the year 200. No mention is made of Heb., 1,2 Pt., 3 Jn., and Jas. The Chester Beatty papyri (P^{45}, P^{46}, P^{47})—first half of third century—contain all the New Testament writings except the Catholic Epistles. It may be seen that Jas., 2 Pt., 2,3 Jn., and Jude were not accepted immediately, while Heb. and Ap. encountered some opposition in the West and East respectively.

In fact we find that the attitude towards these books varied in the great churches: Greek, Latin, and Syriac. The Greeks tended to distinguish books which were "received by all" from books which were "questioned," the latter being Jas., Jude, 2 Pt., and 2,3 Jn. The Johannine authorship, and consequently the canonicity, of Ap. was frequently contested. However, in the second half of the fourth century, Cyril of Jerusalem, the Council of Laodicea, and Gregory Nazianzen testify to the full canon, minus Ap.; while Basil, Gregory of Nyssa, and Epiphanius include the latter also. Athanasius, in 367, enumerates all 27 books, and it may be said that, from this time, the canon was fixed. The canonicity of Ap., although discussed by some theologians in the fifth and sixth centuries, was eventually accepted without question, partly under the influence of the West where there was never any doubt about it.

The churches of the West were, on the whole, faithful in retaining the books which had been confided to them as coming from Apostles, but they made some difficulty about accepting as canonical those whose apostolic origin was not apparent. From Cyprian and Tertullian we learn that Heb., Jas., and 2 Pt. were not part of the collection of the African Church towards the middle of the third century. Furthermore our evidence supports the view that, at this time, the same was true throughout Latin Christendom. In the fourth century the evidence shows that the authority of Heb. and the Catholic Epistles was being more and more recognized in the West—at the very time that Ap. was a subject of discussion in the Greek Church. The Latin canon was, as we have seen, confirmed in Africa by the

Councils of Hippo and Carthage, and in Italy by the letter of Innocent I to Exsuperius.

The Syrian Church of the first centuries was, in part, Greek-speaking, with its center at Antioch; and, in part, Syriac-speaking, with its center at Edessa; the attitude to the New Testament writings was not the same in each area. At Antioch, by the end of the second century, the collection of New Testament books included all except 2 Pt., 2,3 Jn., and Jude. A century later the authority of Ap. was contested; and 2 Pt., 2,3 Jn., and Ap. did not appear in the fifth-century canon of Antioch. In the sixth century there was a reaction in favor of Ap., and later the shorter epistles were accepted. St. John Damascene (d. 754) had the complete canon.

In Edessa the situation was different. Towards the end of the second century, Tatian, a disciple of Justin, made a harmony of the four Gospels in Greek, the Diatessaron—*to dia tessarōn* (*euaggelion*) —which he translated into Syriac about the year 172. It was adopted as the official text at Edessa, and remained the official text until it was supplanted by the Peshitto. At the beginning of the fifth century, the Peshitto became the official text; and Jas., 1 Pt., and 1 Jn. entered the Syriac canon. When, after the Councils of Ephesus (431) and Chalcedon (451), the Syrian Church divided into two heretical sects, the Nestorians remained faithful to the incomplete canon of the Peshitto, while the Monophysites also accepted 2 Pt., Jude, 2,3 Jn., and Ap.

Although the Latin Church canon was fixed in the fifth century, we find that doubts were raised in some quarters respecting the apostolic origin of many writings of the New Testament (Heb., Jas., 2 Pt., 2,3 Jn.). Discussions regarding Heb. persisted into the Middle Ages and final doubts were allayed only by the authority of Thomas Aquinas and Nicholas of Lyra who maintained that the epistle was Pauline. In the sixteenth century the question was raised once more. Erasmus (d. 1536) found himself censured by the theologians of the Sorbonne for querying the apostolic origin of Heb., Jas., 2 Pt., 2,3 Jn., and Ap.—although he did not deny their canonicity. Cardinal Cajetan (d. 1534) held much the same view. Today almost all scholars agree that Heb. and 2 Pt. were not written by Apostles and that the author of Jas. is not the Apostle of the same name; while the authenticity of Jn., Ap., and certain of the Pauline epistles is widely questioned. We must look at the criterion of canonicity.

4. THE CRITERION OF CANONICITY

We have seen that the ultimate criterion of canonicity is the infallible declaration of the Church. Now we must ask how the Church became aware of the inspiration of certain books, and then consider what factor or factors influenced her decision. Since inspiration is a supernatural truth, the fact of the inspiration of each book had to be revealed. There is no trace of explicit revelation regarding the sacred character of each book; otherwise there could have been no difficulty about the deuterocanonical books.

What does follow from the history of the formation of the canon is that the Church was guided in part by the practice and teaching of Christ and his Apostles who certainly regarded the Old Testament as inspired. Historical research suggests that, in deciding which New Testament books are inspired, it is to the principle of apostolicity that the Church had recourse. Any particular book coming from an Apostle, or given with the apostolic guarantee, would be known by revelation to be inspired. But the criterion invoked by the Fathers is not always the apostolic origin of the books. They sometimes regard the Apostles not as the authors of the books, but as the first link in the chain of tradition which finds its expression in the books. It seems that the criterion of canonicity should be understood in the following manner.

Some have suggested that the apostolic character of a New Testament writer would of itself be a sufficient guarantee that the book is inspired. But, besides the fact that this criterion is very hard to apply to the Old Testament, it does not seem justified even for the New. Of course it contains an element of truth. The Church actually did establish the canon of the New Testament by such considerations: she kept the books which came to her from the Apostles and from disciples of the Apostles, and she rejected the others. But for the Church herself this historical consideration was only a human and contingent preliminary to her dogmatic decision, an investigation in the natural order which was as different from her declaration of faith as are the schemata and discussions of a council from the resultant infallible definition. The fact is that, between the stage of human inquiry and that of dogmatic promulgation, there intervenes the action of the Holy Spirit, which guarantees the defined truth against all error. Thus consideration of the prophetic or apostolic character of an author can be at most, even for the Church, only a criterion of the natural order and one which is extrinsic to the dogma of inspiration.[4]

Therefore, when the nonapostolicity of a New Testament writing is critically proved, the decision of the Church is in no way affected, even though the writing was accepted as canonical because it was believed to have been apostolic. The human, historical consideration is contingent, and quite outside the dogmatic decision.

The sole objective and adequate criterion is to be sought in the revelation made by the Holy Spirit to the Church; and the Church, animated and vivified by the Spirit, reads and interprets the Bible through the eyes of the divine Author. While guarding and protecting the Scripture, the Church does not see it only as something to be preserved; rather she finds in it the perfect expression of her own thought. For it is always the thought of the same Spirit of Christ, which he has fixed in the sacred books and renews from age to age in the Church, which he guides.[5]

5. APPENDIX: THE QUMRAN SCROLLS

In the course of this chapter we have mentioned the writings of the Essene community of Qumran (the Dead Sea Scrolls). In view of the interest they have aroused, we think it helpful to give a brief description of these writings as well as a word or two about the men who wrote them.

1) *Discovery of the Scrolls*

In 1947, Cave I was discovered by a young Bedouin shepherd named Mohammed ed-Di'b. Three of the seven manuscripts found in the cave were later acquired by E. L. Sukenik whose complete edition appeared posthumously in 1954; the three were: Is^b, M, H.[6] The other four were in the possession of Mar Athanasius Yeshue Samuel, Syrian Metropolitan of St. Mark's Monastery, Jerusalem. The American School of Oriental Research published (1950-51) three of them:

---

[4]Paul Synave and Pierre Benoit, *La Prophétie* (Tournai: Desclée, 1947), pp. 296 f.; English edition, *Prophecy and Inspiration*, trans. Avery R. Dulles and Thomas L. Sheridan (New York: Desclee, 1961), p. 150.

[5]See A. Robert and A. Feuillet, *Introduction à la Bible* (Tournai: Desclée, 1957), I, p. 45.

[6]These *sigla*, which are explained in the course of the appendix, are normally preceded by the letter "Q," indicating "Qumran," and a digit indicating the cave of origin. Thus 4Q means Qumran, cave 4.

Is^a, p Hab, S. The four manuscripts of Mar Samuel were bought by the State of Israel; since 1955 all the manuscripts of Cave I have been in the Hebrew University, Jerusalem. The seventh scroll (1Q Apoc.) was published in 1956.

In February of 1952, the Ta'amireh Bedouins found fragmentary manuscripts in Cave II. In March the École Biblique, the American School, and the Palestinian Museum carried out an examination of the cliffs for five miles around Qumran and discovered only one cave with manuscript fragments: Cave III. (This cave contained the copper scroll.) In September, the Bedouins discovered the very important Cave IV, which held about 25,000 fragments of more than 400 manuscripts. At this time also, Caves V and VI were found. In 1955, Caves VII-X yielded a few fragments. In 1956, the Bedouins discovered Cave XI, with manuscripts comparable in importance to those of Caves I and IV. In 1951 and 1952, manuscripts had been found at Wadi Murabba'at, farther south; these date from the Second Jewish Revolt, 132-135 A.D.

The manuscript material from all the caves except IQ is in the Palestinian Museum, Jerusalem (Jordan). It is being published in the series, *Discoveries in the Judaean Desert* (O.U.P.); to date, three volumes have appeared.

2) *The Qumran Library*[7]

So far the caves of Qumran have produced parts of almost 600 manuscripts, but only about ten scrolls have been preserved complete, and some texts are represented by one fragment only. All are from a period of about 300 years: between the third century B.C. and the first century A.D.

BIBLICAL   A quarter of the manuscripts consists of copies of
MANUSCRIPTS   books of the Bible. All the books of the Hebrew canon are attested except Est.; many, like Dt., Is., the minor prophets, and Ps. are represented by more than ten copies.

Pentateuch. The majority of the manuscripts of the *Pentateuch* represent the Masoretic, or standardized, Hebrew text (MT). However, 4QEx^a, 4QNm^b, and 4QDt32 are close to the Hebrew text

---

[7]See J. T. Milik, *Ten Years of Discovery in the Wilderness of Judaea* (Naperville, Ill.: Allenson, 1959), pp. 20-43.

underlying the LXX, while 4QEx^b and some readings of 4QNm^b are close to the Samaritan *Pentateuch*.

Former Prophets. Very important is 4QSm^a, whose fragments give examples of every chapter of the work; it is closely related to the Greek Septuagint text (LXX). The extremely fragmentary 4QSm^b represents a text superior to LXX and MT and, dated to the end of the third century B.C., is the oldest known biblical manuscript.

Latter Prophets. These are abundantly represented; especially Is. 1QIs^b (incomplete) represents very faithfully the MT tradition. 1QIs^a (complete) is a text of a popular type, yet one very close to MT. Ezek. and the minor prophets follow MT; 4QJer^b follows the LXX.

Writings. On the whole, these manuscripts follow MT, with some variants. Job is represented by two manuscripts: one in the normal square characters; the other in paleo-Hebraic script; it is likely that the original of the book was written in the latter script. Extensive fragments of an Aramaic translation of Job were found in Cave XI. There are a dozen fragmentary scrolls of Psalms, some of which, however, never contained more than Ps. 119 (118), written out stichometrically and alphabetically. (It seems that a complete scroll of Ps. was found in 11Q.) Seven manuscripts represent Daniel, and the text is identical with MT. The transition from Hebrew to Aramaic is given just as we know it.

The d-c books. Tb., Sir., and Letter of Jeremiah are represented. Three of the manuscripts of Tb. are in Aramaic and one is in Hebrew; Milik suggests that Aramaic was the original language. Both the Aramaic and Hebrew texts correspond to the long recension of Codex Sinaiticus and Vetus Latina, and they emphasize the superiority of the Vetus Latina. Among the fragments of Cave II a few scraps of the Hebrew original of Sir. (6:20-31) have been identified; they are practically identical with the Cairo Geniza manuscripts. Small fragments of papyrus found in Cave VII give part of the Letter of Jeremiah in Greek.

OLD TESTAMENT A sizable section of the Qumran manuscripts rep-
PSEUDEPIGRAPHA resent Pseudepigrapha of the Old Testament.

The Book of Jubilees. This book tells again the story of salvation, from the Creation until the theophany of Sinai. The account of the origins of the Chosen People is given in periods of 49 years and the number of periods itself is 49, so that the whole forms a Jubilee of Jubilees. The author's aim is to find, especially in the story of the Patriarchs, justification for the laws and customs of his time. Caves I, II, and IV have produced fragments of about ten manuscripts of this work. Its Hebrew text corresponds closely to the archetype presupposed by the (complete) Ethiopic and (incomplete) Latin versions. The insistence on a special form of solar calendar and on fixed dates for the main festivals—both important characteristics of the Qumran sect—suggests that, in this case, the work was itself written by a member of the sect; historical allusions make it probable that its composition occurred well before 100 B.C.

The *Book of Enoch* is represented by about ten fragmentary manuscripts from Cave IV—the language is Aramaic. Four of the five parts found in the Ethiopic version are represented; the absence of fragments from the second part, the "Similitudes" on the Son of Man, must be noted: it can scarcely be the work of chance. The "Similitudes" are probably to be considered the work of a Jew or a Jewish Christian of the first or second century A.D. (Milik).

The *Testaments of the Twelve Patriarchs*. Fragments from Caves I and IV belong to an Aramaic *Testament of Levi*. Another fragment (Heb.) represents the *Testament of Naphtali*. These seem to be the sources of the complete work which is a Christian compilation.

The *Genesis Apocryphon* from Cave I (1QApoc.): Aramaic. This book can be described as a legendary paraphrase of Genesis.

4Q *Prayer of Nabonidus*: Aramaic. Its text runs as follows:

> The words of the prayer made by Nabonidus, king of (Assyria and of) Babylon, (the great) king, (when he was smitten) with a malignant disease, by the decree of the (Most High God, in the town of) Teima: "I was smitten (with a malignant disease) for a period of seven years, and became unlike (men. But when I had confessed my sins) and faults, God vouchsafed me a magician. He was a Jew from among (those exiled in Babylon). He gave his explanation and wrote an order that honor and (great glory) should be given to the Name of the (Most High God. And thus he wrote: 'While) you were smitten with a (malignant) disease (in the town of) Teima (by decree of the Most High God), you prayed for seven years (to gods) of silver and gold, (of bronze, iron) wood, stone, clay. . . .'"

This account, which contains certain historical elements (Nabonidus, the last neo-Babylonian king, and his stay of approximately seven years in the oasis of Teima), seems to be the source used, either in an oral or a written form, by the author of the Book of Daniel when he is writing of Nebuchadnezzar's illness. Beneath his pen the name of the great king displaces that of Nabonidus; Teima is replaced by the more illustrious Babylon; and the illness, although still lasting seven years, acquires features unknown to medical science.

SECTARIAN   The *Damascus Document* (CD). This document was
LITERATURE   discovered in Cairo (two manuscripts) in 1897, and was published in 1910. Fragments of it were found in Caves IV, V, and VI. The founder of the sect of the New Covenant was a certain "Teacher of Righteousness" who lived in the time of Antiochus IV (175-163 B.C.). Because of the hostility of the high priest, the group, or part of it, retired to Damascus (Qumran?). The document is the rule and program of life of the sect.

The *Rule of the Community* (1QS) (*Manual of Discipline*). This manuscript is very closely related to CD. It is the rule of the Essenian community of Qumran, and is represented by a complete scroll (1Q) and ten fragmentary manuscripts from Cave IV.

The *Thanksgiving Hymns* (1QH)—also represented by fragments from Cave IV. They comprise five hymns similar to the psalms of the Psalter.

The *Rule for the War* (1QM) (The War of the Sons of Light and the Sons of Darkness)—also fragments of five manuscripts from Cave IV. The "sons of light" are the sons of Levi, Juda, and Benjamin encamped in the desert of Juda under the leadership of the Zadokite priests. Their adversaries are the "sons of darkness," the disciples of Belial. The book is a sort of battle manual containing a victory song and thanksgiving canticles. It is one of the latest works of the Qumran community.

The *copper rolls from Cave III*. This is a text consisting of twelve columns engraved on three sheets of metal that were originally riveted together. The whole roll is 2.4 meters long. It contains a list of about sixty deposits of treasure, hidden in various sites scattered over the Palestinian countryside, but mainly concentrated in the region of Jerusalem, near the Temple and in the cemetery of the Kedron valley. The total of gold and silver said to be buried exceeds 6,000 talents (200 tons).

COMMENTARIES ON The biblical commentaries of the Essenes have
BIBLICAL BOOKS a uniform pattern. The biblical text is transcribed and then commented upon, verse by verse, the comment
being introduced by a formula such as "The explanation (*pesher*)
of this is . . ."; or "The explanation of this word is. . . ." Hence we
call them *pesharim*, that is, "explanations."

The *Commentary on Habakkuk* (1QpHab.). There are also *pesharim* on Nahum (4QpNah.), Isaiah, Micah, Psalms, and Hosea.

4Q *Testimonia*. This is a florilegium of Messianic texts: Dt. 5:25 f.;
18:18 f.; Nm. 24:15 f.; Dt. 33:8-11; plus a quotation from the
apocryphal *Psalms of Joshua*.

3) *The Essenes of Qumran*

The Essenes are a development or branch of the *Hasidim* (the
"pious ones"), a Jewish party noted for their attachment to the Law.
Before the Maccabees, they resisted the pagan influence and then
supported the Maccabean revolt (1 Mc. 2:42; 2 Mc. 14:6), while
maintaining their own freedom of action (1 Mc. 7:13). Later they
repudiated the policy of the Hasmoneans and split into two branches:
Pharisees and Essenes. The phases of Essene history may be recon-
structed by means of archaeological data and indications in their
writings.

The excavation of Khirbet Qumran (five campaigns [1951-56]
carried out by Roland de Vaux, O.P., Director of the École Biblique)
has disclosed three main phases of occupation—the first two by the
Essenes. The whole period of occupation by the sect is well-delineated
by coins. The earliest of these belong to the reign of John Hyrcanus
I (134-104 B.C.); occupation probably began somewhat earlier, as
a protest against the assumption of the high priesthood by Jonathan
(160-142 B.C.).

PHASE ONE 152 B.C.: Jonathan was named high priest by Alexander
Balas. About the year 150 B.C., we find the exodus of the Essenes
to Qumran, led by the Teacher of Righteousness. The monastery, with
its agricultural colony at Ain Feshkha, two and one-half miles south,
supported a community of almost two hundred.

From coins of Herod the Great (37-4 B.C.), which are the last
precisely datable evidence from this level, De Vaux connects the

destruction of Qumran with the earthquake of 31 B.C. related by Josephus. The first period of occupation, then, was from 150-31 B.C.

PHASE TWO   The second phase of occupation began, after a period of abandonment, in the time of Herod's son, Archelaus (4 B.C.-6 A.D.) and, from the evidence of coins, continued to the second year of the Jewish revolt (68 A.D.). Hence about 4 B.C. Essene reconstruction began. The second period of occupation, then, goes from 4 B.C. to 68 A.D.

Now the movement began to spread (that is, from the beginning of the first century A.D.); elsewhere in Palestine and Syria groups were formed; in some of these, marriage (forbidden at Qumran) was permitted. Philo and Josephus speak of 4,000 Essenes. But the monastery of Qumran remained the center of the sect until the hour of disaster.

> In the early summer of 68 A.D., the troops of the Xth Legion, whose object was to take Jerusalem on the flank, advanced towards the Dead Sea along the Jordan valley. At first very carefully, then with feverish haste, the monks placed their great treasure, their library, out of harm's way. They were able to save their books, but not their lives. A breach in the wall, traces of fire, some Roman arrowheads—these are silent witnesses of what took place. The brethren must have been wiped out to the last man in that year 68 for, if even one of them had escaped, the caves would not have preserved their secret to our day.[8]

---

[8] J. Jeremias, "Qumrân et la Théologie," *Nouvelle Revue Théologique*, 85 (1963), 678 f.

| EIGHT | *The Text of the Bible* |

THE LANGUAGES OF THE BIBLE
THE MANUSCRIPTS
THE GREEK AND LATIN VERSIONS

Today we have reached the stage when we can be sure that a version of Scripture, made by competent scholars, is a faithful rendering of the original languages of the Bible. However, there is a qualification which goes beyond the inevitable shortcomings of even the most careful translation: we cannot always be certain that we possess the exact original text, and not a single fragment of the first manuscript of any book exists to reassure us. The object of this chapter is to show that, notwithstanding—because of the abundance of manuscript material—our critical editions of the Bible and the translations based on them do confidently offer us the authentic word of God.

1. THE LANGUAGES OF THE BIBLE

1) *Hebrew*

The language of the Israelites was named "Hebrew" only in the second century B.C. Nehemiah, in the fifth century, speaks of "Judean" (Neh. 13:24), while in the classical age of the eighth century Isaiah called the national language the "language of Canaan" (Is. 19:18). This last designation gives the clue to the origin of the language: Abraham and his descendants, who settled in Canaan, adopted the language of the Canaanites, one that was closely akin to their own. Or it may be—and this seems more likely—that the language of Canaan was adopted after Joshua's conquest; this follows the law by which a military victor succumbs to the higher culture of the conquered.

Hebrew, one of the West-Semitic group of languages, is not confined to the Bible. The Qumran manuscripts show that the language had been revived, at least to this limited extent (and more likely as a written language only), a little before the Christian era. This already marked an evolution towards the Hebrew of the *Mishnah*.[1] The later rabbinical Hebrew of the Middle Ages is to biblical Hebrew as scholastic Latin is to the classical language. This Hebrew, further developed, has become in our time the official and spoken language of the State of Israel.

2) *Aramaic*

Before the establishment of Israel in Canaan, Assyrian documents mention the existence of nomadic and sedentary tribes called Arameans. Although they never attained political unity, their language spread from Syria into the whole of the Middle East. In this entire area the native language disappeared in the face of Aramaic; at least, Aramaic was accepted as the language of diplomacy and business. The Hebrews, who had adopted the language of Canaan, did not escape the influence of Aramaic. At the end of the eighth century only the nobility understood Aramaic; the common people knew only Hebrew (2 Kgs. 18:26). The Exile marked a turning point, and Ezra's efforts in the fifth century on behalf of Hebrew prove that the language was in difficulties. In the second century, although there was a flourishing apocalyptic literature in Hebrew, the Scripture readings in the synagogue had to be translated into Aramaic; this was the origin of the *Targums* or interpretations, which were eventually preserved in written form. By the time of Christ there were even dialectal variations in the language of the people.

The following texts of the Old Testament were written in Aramaic: Ez. 4:8–6:18; 7:12-26; Dn. 2:4b–7:28; Jer. 10:11; two words in Gn. 31:47. Besides these, there are Aramaisms in some of the later books. And Aramaic, the language of Jesus and his disciples, underlies the Gospels and other parts of the New Testament.

3) *Greek*

Wisdom, 2 Maccabees, the deuterocanonical parts of Esther and Daniel (Est. 10:4–6:24; Dn. 3:24-90; 13-14), and the whole of the

---

[1]The *Mishnah* ("teaching") is the name given to the collection of oral teaching of the earlier rabbis. It was compiled about 200 A.D. Together with the *Gemara* (commentary on the *Mishnah* and later traditions) it forms the Talmud, which might be described as the oral Torah, or ensemble of authoritative traditions.

New Testament, are written in Greek, but, and this is true particularly of the New Testament, in a language that differs widely from classical Greek. For a long time this biblical Greek was thought to be artificial —and as original as the religious ideas it expresses. Thanks in large measure to the discovery, in Egypt, of many nonliterary texts written on papyrus in the language of everyday life, the problem has been clarified. The accepted view may be summarized as follows:

1. The language of the Bible is *Koine* Greek, that is, the language which from the time of Alexander the Great became the *lingua franca* of the Eastern Mediterranean. Since it was a common language, spoken by different peoples, simplicity was a necessity. Therefore the grammar became more and more uniform and difficult forms were dropped. At the same time new words were introduced.

2. On the whole, biblical Greek is *popular* Koine Greek. With Heb. a notable exception, almost all the New Testament is written in the language of everyday life: the same language as that of the Egyptian papyri.

3. Biblical Greek bears the imprint of the Semitic mind and was much influenced by Hebrew and Aramaic. Indeed this influence is inevitable, since the authors of the Old Testament books and sections were Jews, and since Aramaic was the mother tongue of all the New Testament writers, except Luke. At the same time, the Bible of the early Church, the Septuagint, preserved the strong flavor of its Hebrew original.

2. THE MANUSCRIPTS

1) *Hebrew*

We have seen that the Hebrew canon was fixed at the end of the first century A.D. The common view, that the text also was fixed at the same time, has been reinforced by the evidence of the Qumran and Murabba'at biblical texts.[2] However, the work of the Masoretes (600-1,000 A.D.) was of prime importance. These scholars set out to restore and to stabilize the text. To do so they annotated the manuscripts, placing the notes in the margins. The collection of notes was called *massora* ("tradition"). No changes were made in the text, and proposed corrections were indicated as follows: the word to be changed was marked with a masoretic circle or asterisk and was called

---

[2]See p. 74.

kethib ("written"); the correction was indicated in the margin and was called *qere* ("to be read"). The Masoretes invented, and inserted in the text, a system of vowel-points; for the Hebrew alphabet, like that of other Semitic languages, is consonantal only. The Hebrew text, finally established by the Masoretes, is called the Masoretic Text (MT).

Until the sensational and utterly unexpected Qumran discoveries, our earliest Hebrew manuscripts did not antedate the last decade of the ninth century A.D. The most important are:

1. *Pentateuch* (Gn. 39:20-Dt. 1:33): tenth century; British Museum.
2. *Codex Prophetarum*: 895; Cairo.
3. *Codex Petropolitanus*: tenth century; Leningrad.

The last is the basis of the third and later critical editions of Kittel. P. Kahle has established that it is a good copy of the Codex of the Sephardite synagogue in Aleppo, dated about 950.

The fresh elements furnished by the manuscript of Qumran show the history of the Hebrew text under a new light.[3] We have the impression that the rabbis of the "Synod" of Jamnia (90-95 A.D.) possessed very old manuscripts of the Bible. Their method of editing was largely mechanical, or so we are led to believe; for, according to the *Mishnah*, they consulted the three manuscripts of the Torah, formerly preserved in the Temple, and selected the readings of two against the third. The same method was likely used for the other books. Perhaps, by chance, some books, like those of the Former Prophets, were accessible to the editors only in a recension less faithful to the original than that translated in the LXX. The Writings, in our Qumran manuscripts, seem to have been treated very freely; the process of fixing these texts began later. At the same time the Samaritans fixed their canon, which they limited to the *Pentateuch*. When the text of the whole Bible was fixed, the Jews of Palestine almost at once rejected all other recensions and the Greek versions based on earlier texts.

The great importance of the Qumran discoveries, from the point of view of the history of the text, is that they put us in contact with a stage of the textual tradition before the fixing of the text. The biblical fragments of Murabba'at (documents hidden during the second revolt, 132-35 A.D.), and another lot of unknown origin, present

---

[3]See J. T. Milik, *Ten Years of Discovery in the Wilderness of Judaea* (Naperville, Ill.: Allenson, 1959), pp. 28 f.

a text that is, at least for the *Pentateuch,* Is., minor prophets, and Ps., identical with the Masoretic Text—which had been fixed in the meantime.

THE SAMARITAN The Samaritan manuscripts of the *Pentateuch* are
PENTATEUCH not earlier than those of the MT; the oldest seems to date to about the twelfth century A.D. The superiority of the Samaritan text was formerly urged; now, however, it is generally admitted that the Samaritan tradition is inferior to that of the MT. But the manner in which the Samaritans of Nablus read their text may be of help; they may have preserved traditional pronunciations, which would suggest alternative interpretations of a group of consonants.

2) *Greek: New Testament*

THE GREEK The oldest manuscripts of the New Testament are
MANUSCRIPTS written in the contemporary script, the uncial—also called maiuscule or capital. The letters were unattached and there was no distinction of words or sentences. Cursive script (smaller script, with letters frequently joined) was in use at an early date, and was employed for nonliterary documents in New Testament times. Later, in the ninth century, the minuscule form was current; this is characterized by smaller, more flowing letters, frequently linked, and with many abbreviations.

Throughout the first two Christian centuries the common writing material was papyrus. Papyrus was a reed-like plant, then abundant in the Nile delta. The pith of the plant was cut into long, thin strips which, laid first vertically and then horizontally, were glued together and the surface was rubbed smooth. The resulting sheets were joined to form a scroll of the desired length or were arranged in book form (codex). From the second century A.D. parchment (originating at Pergamum in Asia Minor) began to compete with papyrus; it was much more durable, and by the fourth century it had ousted papyrus. Parchment could be reused; it was possible to rub or scrape off an earlier text. A parchment so used is called a palimpsest (from the Greek *palin* ["again"] and *psao* ["to rub"]). The original text, usually the more important, can be recovered by a modern chemical and photographic process. In the eighth century paper was introduced from the East, but until the invention of printing the more durable papyrus was preferred for the sacred text.

The extant Greek manuscripts of the New Testament are classified under the headings Papyri, Uncials, Minuscules, and Lectionaries (liturgical texts), and are provided with a special system of reference. The papyri are listed with the letter P followed by an index number in superior type (for example, P^{45}). The uncials are designated by a number with an initial zero (01, 02, etc.); however, for the first 45 uncials, an older system has been preserved: Aleph (S); A-Z; Gamma-Omega. The minuscules are numbered simply 1-2430; and the lectionaries are listed by number, preceded by the letter "1" (for example, 1.2073).

The Papyri. We now have some 75 New Testament papyri. They are of Egyptian origin for the most part. Their importance is due to the fact that (1) some of them are older by 100 to 150 years than our oldest parchment manuscripts; (2) they are an authentic witness of the Egyptian text-form. The most important papyri are:

P^{52}—Rylands papyrus. A codex fragment containing Jn. 18, 31-33; 37-38. Published in 1935 and now in the John Rylands Library, Manchester. It is dated c. 130 A.D.

P^{5}—Fragments of Jn.: third century.

P^{13}—Fragments of Heb.: c. 300. These are among the Oxyrhynchus Papyri published in London, 1892-1927, by Grenfell and Hunt. These papyri are, for the most part, nonbiblical.

The *Chester Beatty papyri*. From 1930-36, A. Chester Beatty got possession of twelve Egyptian papyrus codices, three of which are New Testament codices of the third century. Now in Dublin, they are:

P^{45}—30 fragmentary pages of a codex that contained the four Gospels and Acts, in the following order: Mt., Jn., Lk., Mk., Acts.

P^{46}—86 pages of a codex that originally had 104 pages; it contains the Pauline epistles (including Heb. but minus the Pastorals).

P^{47}—10 fragmentary pages of a codex of the Ap.

P^{66}—*Papyrus Bodmer II*. Published by V. Martin, Geneva, 1956. It contains the Gospel of St. John from the Prologue to 14:26. It is dated c. 200, and as such is about a century earlier than the Chester Beatty papyri. (The only earlier text we have is P^{52}.) It appears to have been of Egyptian origin. The text of Papyrus Bodmer II is very close to our critical text (for example, Nestle).

The Uncials. We possess 212 uncial manuscripts, or fragments of manuscripts, written on parchment. The most important are:

B—Codex Vaticanus: fourth century; now in the Vatican Library. It contains the entire Old Testament, and the New Testament to Heb. 9:14a. (The Pastorals, Philemon and Ap. are missing, but were originally included.)

א (S)—Codex Sinaiticus: fourth century. It was discovered by Tischendorff in the monastery of St. Catherine on Mt. Sinai (1844-59); then it was taken to Leningrad, and in 1933 bought by the British Museum for £100,000. It contains nearly half of the Old Testament and the entire New Testament, plus the *Epistle of Barnabas* and the *Pastor of Hermas.*

A—Codex Alexandrinus: fifth century. Most likely of Egyptian origin, in 1628 it was presented to Charles I of England by the Patriarch Cyril Lukaris of Constantinople; it is now in the British Museum. It contains the Old Testament and the New Testament, with some serious gaps. It also has the two epistles of Clement.

C—Codex Ephraemi rescriptus: fifth century. Of Egyptian origin, it is now in the Bibliothèque Nationale, Paris. It is a palimpsest and was used in the twelfth century for a Greek version of several of St. Ephrem's works. Originally containing the whole Bible, it now consists of no more than small portions of the Old Testament and about two-thirds of the New Testament.

D—(ev. act.) Codex Bezae or Cantabrigiensis: fifth or sixth century. It is the oldest of the bilingual (Greek and Latin) codices. It was at Lyons from the ninth century until 1562, when the Huguenots took it from the monastery of St. Irenaeus and gave it to Theodore of Beza, a disciple and friend of Calvin. In 1581, he presented it to Cambridge University, where it is now preserved. In Greek and Latin it contains the four Gospels (Mt., Jn., Lk., Mk.) almost intact, and Acts with gaps; plus some fragments of 3 Jn. and Ap.

W—Codex Freerensis: fifth century. Bought in Egypt in 1906 by

C. L. Freer, it is now in Washington. It contains, with some gaps, the four Gospels (Mt., Jn., Lk., Mk.). After Mk. 16:14 there is an addition, the so-called Freer Logion.

Θ—The Codex Koridethi: seventh to the ninth centuries. It is now in Tiflis (Tbilisi, Georgia). In the marginal notes there is frequent mention of Koridethi in the Caucasus. It contains, almost in entirety, the four Gospels.

D—(Paul.) Codex Claromontanus: sixth century. Bought from the monastery of Clermont by Theodore of Beza, it is now in the Bibliothèque Nationale, Paris. It is bilingual and contains, with some gaps, the Pauline epistles (including Heb.).

The Minuscules. There are more than 2,400 minuscule manuscripts, or fragments. While it is true that the majority of them have little or no critical value, still there are numerous notable exceptions. The minuscules have not yet been used to full advantage; the comparatively recent date of these codices has been against them from the first. They do not date from before the ninth century; hence they are much later than the fourth- or fifth-century uncials. For this reason they are judged inferior. Today it is recognized that a late codex may present an excellent text if it is the transcription of a much older codex. Recently, therefore, the minuscule manuscripts are receiving more critical treatment. An attempt has been made to collate them and to classify them according to their proper families.

Research has shown that the manuscripts (including uncials) may be arranged according to families. The term is explained by F. G. Kenyon: "If in a given manuscript of any work some words are wrongly transcribed, or a passage omitted, every manuscript copy from it, or from copies of it, will have the same mistakes or the same omissions; and if among the extant manuscripts we find that several have the same important mistake or omission, it is legitimate to argue that they are all descended from the manuscripts in which that mistake or omission was first made."[4] Thus we can assign the various manuscripts to different families or groups, with characteristic types of readings. This is how the recensions have been identified.

---

[4] *The Text of the Greek Bible* (Naperville, Ill.: Allenson, 1958²), p. 11.

1) Family 13, or the Ferrar group, comprises a dozen manuscripts (ϕ in E. Nestle).[5]

2) Family 1, brought together by K. Lake, contains a half dozen manuscripts (λ in E. Nestle). This is closely connected, not only with Family 13, but also with certain uncials, notably W.

461 is the oldest minuscule. It bears the date, May 7, 835.

> Only about 50 of these codices originally contained the whole New Testament. As in the case of the uncials, the greater part of them have the Gospels only, while the Ap. as usual is represented less frequently than any other book. On the other hand, they contain, oftener than the uncials, various kinds of accessory matters, such as a list of the seventy disciples, biographies of the Apostles, a summary of St. Paul's journeys, etc., which are a slight indication of a less ancient origin.[6]

The Lectionaries. We possess about 2000 lectionaries, that is, manuscripts containing the portions of the New Testament that were read publicly during the divine service, or, simply, liturgical books. Apart from a few fragments on papyrus, they are uncial or semi-uncial manuscripts. These are of comparatively recent date, the oldest, very few in number, not going back beyond the sixth century. They differ according to the ecclesiastical provinces whence they derive. They seem to have been responsible for a certain number of variants in the semi-uncials and even in the uncials. At the same time, due account must be taken of the conservative tendency of the liturgy. Thus the script remains uncial, sometimes as late as the eleventh century, and great care was taken in the transcription of these books; the text itself sometimes gives us very old readings. Hence they are not without interest.

Citations in the Fathers. The value of citations in the early Fathers is that (1) they enable us to determine the text in use in a particular time and place; and that (2) the writers frequently follow texts that are older than our Greek manuscripts. Thus, for example, from the writings of Cyprian (d. 258), we have an idea of the text that was in use in the African Church in the first half of the third

---

[5]See E. Nestle, *Novum Testamentum Graece*[24] (Stuttgart: Privilegierte Württembergische Bibelanstalt, 1960). This is the most convenient critical edition of the Greek text. Nestle's system of signs is followed here.

[6]L. Vaganay, *Introduction to the Textual Criticism of the New Testament*, trans. B. V. Miller (London: Sands, 1937), p. 31.

century. Since the citations in the patristic writings often differ from the text in our manuscripts, it was commonly held that, in such cases, they are quoting from memory.

Latest research has shown that the Fathers (apart from the earliest Fathers who usually only alluded to Scripture) followed a Bible text much more closely than we had been wont to believe. Hence, when they differ from the text of our manuscripts, they do so because they follow another text, and one that is frequently older and closer to the original. Of particular interest are the occasions when an author draws attention to a number of variants and weighs one against another; for example, Jerome, in his *Epistle 119*, gives three text-forms of 1 Cor. 15:51, and says that one of them is to be found only in the Latin version. Eusebius assures us that the so-called canonical Mark-ending is wanting in the oldest and best manuscripts.[7] This aspect of textual criticism has been rather neglected, but is now receiving due consideration.

PRESENT-DAY POSITION OF THE GREEK TEXT   The Greek manuscripts, then, offer an enormous mass of material; and to them must be added the ancient versions. The study of the whole represents an immense labor, but scholars have gallantly faced up to the task. As a result, four great categories of texts have been established. This has helped to bring order into the crowded field; but some feel that the approach has been oversimplified and that, in fact, much relevant material has not been taken into account at all. We shall summarize the results achieved and then note the latest tendencies.

The Four Principal Text-Forms.[8] 1. The Alexandrian or Neutral Text (Nestle: 𝕳). The existence of this text-form has long been recognized. It is a noticeably *shorter* text, that is, shorter than any of the other text-forms, of which the Western is the longest. It is not a grammatically and stylistically polished text like the Koine and, to a lesser degree, Caesarean texts. According to the opinion of the majority of textual critics, this Neutral text is the best of the known text-forms. The later papyrus and manuscript discoveries (for example, the Chester Beatty papyri) have not substantially increased

---

[7]A. Wikenhauser, *Einleitung in das Neue Testament* (Freiburg: Herder, 1956[2]), pp. 66 f.; English edition, *New Testament Introduction*, trans. Joseph Cunningham (New York: Herder and Herder, 1963), p. 91.

[8]See *ibid.*, pp. 99-109; English edition, pp. 137-49.

the evidence for this form. But they have taught us: (1) that this form was not the only one known in Egypt; (2) that it, or the form on which it is based, goes back to the second century.

The question is whether the Neutral text, as represented by B, is a recension or the result of a particularly faithful textual transmission. It is now commonly held that the Neutral text presents a revision on the basis of ancient manuscripts current in Egypt; but it is a careful revision made by a scholar who wanted to restore the original text. Hort has shown that A and S have, through ancestors that had drawn apart, sprung from the same archetype, which was established in the second century. What was produced about the year 300 was not a new text-type, but a carefully-presented witness of an already existing text.

2. The Western Text. Nestle says: "I am not inclined to use a common sign for the so-called 'Western' text because its representatives differ too much among themselves and are therefore better mentioned individually."

The existence of a special text, differing from the Neutral and Koine, was long admitted. It was called the Western text because it underlay the Old Latin versions, the Greek-Latin manuscripts, and was found in the Latin Fathers before 400. This form has been identified in the Gospels, Acts, and the Pauline epistles. The characteristic notes of the Western text are: (1) notable additions and omissions; (2) free narrative formation, by comparison with the Neutral text. The Western text was early in use. It was employed by Marcion, Irenaeus, Tertullian, and Cyprian. Its chief witness is the Old Latin version of about the year 200.

The questions of the origin and worth of the Western text are still unsolved. Modern textual critics avoid both extreme favorable and unfavorable views. They recognize that the Western text, already found in the middle of the second century, certainly contains some very good, even original, readings, which the Neutral text no longer possesses. For this reason, modern critics are not so exclusively in favor of the Neutral text. The chief witnesses of the Western text are: (1) Gospels: D; 0171; Old Latin; (2) Acts: D; 614; 383; P^{38}, P^{48}; Old Latin; Ephrem; (3) Paul: DEGF (bilingual); Greek Ff to end of 3rd cent.; Old Latin; Syriac Ff to c. 450.

3. The Caesarean Text. The manuscripts W and Theta led to the discovery of this form. It now seems that these manuscripts represent a special text that could not be fitted into the known forms. Then it was discovered that there were other witnesses to the same text: Families 1,13; 28,565,700. This text was used by Origen. P[45] proves that it was known in Egypt in the first half of the third century. It appears that it was brought from Egypt to Caesarea by Origen. According to the latest research of Kirsopp and Silva Lake, we must distinguish two steps in this text:

a) P[45]; W; Families 1,13; 38—these represent the Old Egyptian text which Origen brought to Caesarea (= the pre-Caesarean text).

b)   ; 565,700; Origen, Eusebius; the Georgian versions—the Caesarean text, strictly so called. Similar results have followed from a study of Acts and Paul. Nestle says: "For the Caesarean type of text Theta stands as inclusive representative."

4. The Koine Text (Nestle = К). The late uncials and the great majority of minuscules represent a text that is remarkably uniform. The existence of this form is well known, but its date and place of origin are still disputed.

Westcott and Hort called it the Syrian text because, in the time of Chrysostom, it was used in Syrian Antioch; for the same reason it has been called the Antiochian text. Others called it the Byzantine text because its latest form was the common text of the Eastern Empire. Von Soden named it the Koine text because it became the *textus receptus* or the "accepted text" of the Greek Church. Its characteristics are: literary polish; stylistic touches; minor explanatory additions; and notable harmonization in the Gospels.

The conclusion is that the Koine and Western texts show abundant traces of free editorial revision which is less evident in the Neutral and Caesarean texts. The revision of the former was due to the work of scholarly editors who desired an authentic text rather than an easy one. They are the best available for the recovery of the authentic New Testament text.

The Latest Tendencies.[9] The result of textual criticism has been to establish the Alexandrian text as the best text-form. It is thought

---

[9]See M.-E. Boismard, *Initiation Biblique* (Tournai: Desclée, 1954[3]), pp. 398-401; English edition, *Guide to the Bible*, trans. E. P. Arbez and M. R. P. McGuire (New York: Desclee, 1960[2]), pp. 617-19.

sufficient to edit this, with a certain number of corrections, in order to obtain a text that has the best chance of representing the original biblical text. Thus the critical editions, taken together, produce a text that is very close to the Alexandrian. Such is the commonly accepted position.

Today, many scholars regard this view as an oversimplification of the question. The modern tendencies in textual criticism are the following:

1. It is felt that the field of work has been too much restricted. It is scarcely legitimate to base a critical text almost exclusively on the great uncials. Instead, the importance of the minuscules is being stressed. It is realized, too, that the lectionaries are of importance; and the old versions are being studied to a far greater extent. Especially, biblical citations in the Fathers are receiving close attention; these often have readings older than those of our oldest manuscripts. As a result of all this, the versions and patristic citations probably will gain in value as elements in the search for the primitive text and the absolute supremacy of the uncials will come to an end.

2. The division of the manuscripts into families is being questioned with regard to its utility and even its legitimacy. At the very least, the division is judged to be far too systematic. For example, D is now reckoned as a bad representative of the Western text. Furthermore the Alexandrian text appears not so well-defined as was hitherto believed. One of its "best" representatives, S, is often closer to the Syro-Latin (Western) text than to B. The question is: When one or more witnesses of the Alexandrian text present "Western" readings, is that by contamination? or rather, is it by the conservation of primitive readings common to the Western and Alexandrian texts and later abandoned by B and the others? This last view would affect fundamentally the division of the texts.

3. Thus the tendency is not to judge a variant on the ground of belonging to a particular text-form. Rather it should be judged by internal criteria; no variant should be rejected a priori because it belongs to a rejected text or because it has no support in the uncials. Each variant must be judged on its own merits.

In short, it is still premature to wish to establish a New Testament text that purports to represent as nearly as possible the original. But this is not to say that we cannot use a critically established text with confidence. Although the mass of New Testament manuscripts furnishes us with about 150,000 variants, the majority of these are insignificant—orthographical changes or simple scribal errors. Scholars are agreed that nine-tenths of the text is certain and that the important variants are very few.

3. THE GREEK AND LATIN VERSIONS

The early versions are of great importance in helping to establish the original text. Within our limited scope we cannot give a complete account of them; we shall treat of the Greek and Latin versions only.

1) *The Septuagint (LXX)*

The Jewish colony in Alexandria was a large and important one. The Hellenized Jews wanted a version of the sacred books in Greek. The apocryphal letter of Aristeas to Philocrates (written at the latest in the second century B.C.) tells how, at the request of the king, Ptolemy II Philadelphos (285-246 B.C.), the high priest Eleazar sent 72 elders from Jerusalem to Alexandria in order to translate the Law. They were installed on the Island of Pharos and in 72 days had finished the work. The account of Aristeas is legendary, of course, although it was accepted by Philo, Josephus, Irenaeus, Clement of Alexandria, and many others. But we can assume that the *Pentateuch* was translated first, and that this translation was made during the reign of Ptolemy Philadelphos. The translation of the other books followed. The Prologue of Sirach (c. 130 B.C.) tells us that at that date the "Law, Prophets, and the rest of the books" had been translated into Greek.

Such had been the accepted position until recent discoveries shed new light on the question. It seems that the earliest translations were of liturgical texts, in the style of the Targums; thus there was a series of partial translations. Eventually, the whole Bible was translated for private use.

In 1952 some fragments of the Greek text were found in Qumran (4Q); they date from before the end of the first century A.D. They were fragments of two manuscripts of Lv., one on papyrus and the other on leather. The text is exactly that of the LXX. Therefore this version was known in Palestine in the time of our Lord. Also in 1952 a fragmentary text on leather of the minor prophets was acquired by the Palestine Museum. Dated to the end of the first century A.D., this text is a scholarly revision of the LXX. The fifth column of Origen's *Hexapla* seems to have been based on it.

The LXX is not a uniform translation, but varies from book to book. The *Pentateuch,* and the historical books in general, are most faithful to the original. The Greek is best in Jb., Prv., and in the books originally written in Greek: Wis. and 2 Mc. Dn. was so different from the original that it was rejected and replaced by the version of Theodotion. The LXX is based on a Hebrew text that is older, and often better, than the MT.[10]

The LXX version was made by Jews and for Jews. They were the first to make use of it, especially throughout the Diaspora. The Christian Church took over the LXX and the Greek Fathers used it exclusively. The Scriptural citations in the New Testament for the most part come after the LXX. Mt. alone appears to have made a direct translation, at least in some of his quotations. The other writers sometimes modified the Greek slightly to bring it into closer agreement with the Hebrew.

More than 1,500 manuscripts of the LXX (uncials and minuscules) exist. The earliest and most important uncials are BSAD. The Chester Beatty papyri (3-4 century) give fragments of Gn. 4Q (noted above) gives a first century A.D. text of Lv. P. Rylands 458 has fragments of Dt. dating from the second century B.C., the oldest Greek biblical text.

The Hexapla of Origen.[11] The first to have undertaken a great critical revision of the LXX was Origen, at the beginning of the third century. In order to show the exact relationship of the Hebrew text and the Greek translation, he published a parallel edition of both texts with, also in parallel columns, the later Greek translations. His work comprised six columns—hence the name (although in Ps. there were eight columns):

1. The Hebrew text in Hebrew characters.

2. The Hebrew text in Greek characters.

3. The version of Aquila.

4. The version of Symmachus.

5. The LXX.

6. The version of Theodotion.

---

[10]See p. 83.
[11]See G. Bardy, *Initiation Biblique, op. cit.,* pp. 406-8; English edition, pp. 626-28.

An abridged version, the Tetrapla, omitted the Hebrew and the transliteration of it in Greek. For Ps., Origen had discovered two further Greek versions; thus here the work became an Octapla.

The fifth column was by far the most important, not merely because it contained the LXX, but because, whereas Origen simply reproduced the other texts, he carefully revised the LXX in order to restore it to its original purity, and especially to show clearly its relation to the Hebrew. To do this he had recourse to a system of signs that was currently employed in Alexandria for editions of the profane books. Thus he marked with an obelus (÷) the passages which did not occur in the Hebrew and were added in the Greek; and with an asterisk (*) the passages which, although present in the Hebrew, were missing in the Greek. In each case the close of the passage was marked by a metobelus (⸎). The passages introduced into the fifth column were from the other versions, mostly from Theodotion. In establishing the LXX text he chose variant readings that were supported by the later versions.

The Hexapla was, obviously, a work of considerable volume; the original manuscript was in the library of Caesarea; St. Jerome was able to consult it there at the end of the fourth century. It disappeared, apparently, in the seventh century, when the city was captured by the Saracens. In 1897, Cardinal Mercati published a palimpsest fragment (Ps.) of the Hexapla found in the Ambrosian Library, Milan. The fifth column (the LXX) was frequently copied. Unfortunately, the critical signs were usually omitted. This led to further corruption, since without the signs the additions and omissions of Origen were so many variants. Many manuscripts have preserved, at least in part, the Hexaplar recension of the LXX.

2) *The Versions of Aquila, Theodotion, and Symmachus*

In Jewish circles it was recognized that the LXX differed from the official Hebrew text (fixed about the end of the first century A.D.). The Jews wanted a version closer to the *textus receptus* (the "received text").

AQUILA   A Jewish proselyte, a native of Sinope in Pontus; he flourished in the time of Hadrian (117-138). His version was extremely literal; it attempted to reproduce in Greek the slightest peculiarity of the Hebrew. We possess nothing of this work beyond some fragments contained in writers who have cited the Hexapla, and some passages in a palimpsest found in Cairo.

THEODOTION   According to St. Irenaeus, he was a proselyte of Ephesus who lived at the end of the second century. He did not know Hebrew very well—he sometimes even transcribed what he did not understand. In general he followed the LXX very closely, correcting it here and there in the light of Aquila and the Hebrew. Hence, rather than a new version, his was a recension of the revision of the LXX. We do not know the work of Theodotion well. However, almost all the manuscripts of the LXX contain his Dn. rather than the LXX version.

SYMMACHUS   According to St. Epiphanius, he was a Samaritan who became a Jew under Septimius Severus (193-211). His translation was clear and elegant, but not sufficiently literal. We possess only fragments of this text.

The fragmentary manuscript of the minor prophets (end of the first century A.D.), acquired by the Palestine Museum in 1952, has shed new light on the relationship between the LXX and the versions mentioned above. The new text is a recension of the LXX, which seeks to bring the LXX into closer conformity with the Hebrew. The rabbinic version of Aquila, long recognized as a more literal version (than the LXX) of the Hebrew, frequently agrees with the new text of the minor prophets where that differs from the LXX. This shows that the text of Aquila is not original, but is based on the earlier recension represented by the newly-found fragments. Symmachus too seems to have used this recension, for a number of places can be pointed out where he sides with the new text against the LXX. It can be shown that, where he differs from the new text, it is simply in order to give a better Greek style. Apparently Theodotion also used the early recension.[12]

3) *The Old Latin Versions* (*it*)

The importance of these versions was first recognized only towards the end of the seventeenth century. We possess about 50 manuscripts

---

[12]See D. Barthélemy, "Redécouverte d'un chaînon manquant de l'histoire de la Septante," *Revue Biblique*, 60 (1953), 18-29.

and fragments. The importance of the Old Latin manuscripts as a witness of the text is due:

1. To their antiquity: they date from the second half of the second century. (Tertullian used a Latin version.)

2. To the character of the translation: it is usually slavishly literal; hence it is relatively easy to reconstruct the Greek text on which it is based.

3. To the fact that these versions represent the Western text, which in the second and third century had spread everywhere, East and West.[13]

Two types of Old Latin text have been identified: African and European. In each we find the same popular Latin, often ungrammatical and uncouth, that scandalized St. Augustine. In each the translation is strictly literal, even slavishly so. The differences between the two spring from constant linguistic peculiarities, and from particular readings which must have come from different Greek texts. The relation between the African and European texts is much discussed, but one thing is clear: the African texts are more homogeneous and earlier. Carthage and Northern Italy were the centers of translation, revision, and diffusion of the Old Latin. The chief New Testament witnesses are:

1. The African text: Codex Bobbiensis (k)—4-5 centuries; Codex Palatinus (e)—fifth century; the palimpsest Floriacensis (h)—6-7 centuries.

2. The European text: Codex Vercellensis (a)—fourth century; Codex Veronensis (b)—fourth century; Codex Bezae (d)—fifth century; Codex Claromontanus (d)—sixth century; Palimpsest Bobbiensis (s)—5-6 centuries; Codex Gigas (g or gig)—thirteenth century. We must add that the text of Wis., Sir., Bar., 1,2 Mc., as they occur in the Vulgate, is Old Latin; St. Jerome did not translate these books.

4) *The Vulgate* (*vg*)

THE WORK OF ST. JEROME   About the end of the fourth century, because of the multiplicity of manuscripts, the text of the Old Latin was hopelessly corrupt. The revision of the text in use in the Latin Church became an urgent necessity. The man who faced the problem

---

[13]See A. Tricot, *Initiation Biblique, op. cit.,* pp. 417 f.; English edition, pp. 639 f.

and produced a critical text for general use was the greatest biblical scholar of the early Church, Sophronius Eusebius *Hieronymus*.

St. Jerome was born in Stridon in Dalmatia. He studied grammar and rhetoric at Rome and received his scriptural formation in Antioch (374-379) and Constantinople (379-382). He also fully mastered the Greek language and studied Hebrew too. In the year 382, he became secretary to Pope Damasus. The Pope commissioned him to undertake a revision of the Latin version. In 384, St. Jerome dedicated his revision of the four Gospels to the Pope (see the letter in Nestle). In his Preface he complains of many errors in the contemporary texts due to harmonizing tendencies. His work was a revision, not a new translation. He used a relatively good Latin text and revised it according to the Greek; and the Greek text he followed was the Alexandrian as represented by BS. Jerome was careful to preserve the Old Latin idiom wherever that was possible; thus his revision would be more readily acceptable.

It is disputed whether St. Jerome revised the other New Testament books; some deny that he did. According to Wikenhauser, he did revise the other New Testament books, but not as carefully or as radically as the Gospels. Pope Damasus died in December, 384. In August, 385, St. Jerome left Rome, and in 386 he settled in Bethlehem. While he had been working on the Gospels, Jerome also had revised the Psalter according to the LXX—but *cursim*. This text is preserved in the *Commentarioli* of St. Jerome. It is *not* the so-called Roman Psalter found in the Missal and which is used in the Divine Office at St. Peter's (and Milan): this is Old Latin.[14] He made a second revision of the Psalter in Bethlehem (387-388), this time with reference to the Hexapla. This is the "Gallican Psalter," the psalter incorporated in the Vulgate. At the same time, Jb., Chr., Prv., and Sir. were revised according to the Hexapla. Only the text of Jb. is extant.

Jerome did not continue the task of revising the Old Testament; he had decided to produce a new version from the Hebrew original. He translated the protocanonical books from the Hebrew with reference to an Old Latin text, to the LXX, and to the versions of Aquila, Symmachus, and Theodotion (he found these in the Hexapla of Origen). It is not clear whether he translated the deuterocanonical

---

[14]See *ibid.*, p. 426; English edition, p. 649.

parts of Esther from the LXX and those of Dn. from Theodotion, or whether he revised the Old Latin version of these parts with reference to the Greek.

His translation of the Old Testament was accomplished between 391-405. Note two things carefully:

1. Of the d-c books he translated only Tb. and Jdt.—from the Aramaic.

2. The translation of Psalms—*Psalterium Hebraicum* or *ex Hebraeo* —is not incorporated into the Vulgate. It is found in Migne, *PL* 28. The "Gallican Psalter" is found in the Vulgate (and Breviary).

The Vulgate thus comprises:

1. Old Testament: (a) p-c books: Psalter—revision of the Old Latin according to the Hexapla. All the rest are translated from the Hebrew.

b) d-c books: Tb. and Jdt.—translated from the Aramaic; parts of Est. and Dn.—revised according to the LXX and Theodotion, or translated from the LXX and Theodotion. All the rest are from the Old Latin.

2. New Testament. Gospels—revision of the Old Latin according to the Greek. All the rest—revision of the Old Latin according to the Greek or Old Latin.

THE QUALITY OF   St. Jerome's work is always good, but he does
THE VULGATE   not always strike his best form. Sometimes, due
to the pressure of his work, his translation was hasty. Thus he tells us himself that he translated Tb. in one day, and Jdt. was one night's work! But these are the exceptions.

His method was to purify the Latin text of the Bible, and the only means to do that was by the "return to the sources," that is, to the originals as represented by the best Greek manuscripts. With regard to textual criticism, Jerome followed Origen. However, he underestimated the value of the LXX. In his translation, Jerome sometimes exaggerated the messianic sense of a passage, or read a messianic sense into a text. Sometimes, too, his choice of variants was dictated by dogmatic preoccupations. But all this is relatively rare. Not the least quality of Jerome's work is that it is a literary masterpiece. Jerome, like Augustine, was a master of Latin prose in the Christian era. In short, thanks to the genius of St. Jerome, the Western Church was endowed with an edition of the Bible that was a worthy successor to the LXX. The work of St. Jerome was eventually declared the official version of the Latin Church.

The most noteworthy Vulgate manuscripts are: (1) Amiatinus (A): Northumberland—7-8 centuries, Florence; (2) Fuldensis (F): Fulda —sixth century; Mediolanensis (M): sixth century, Milan; (3) Harleianus (Z): 6-7 centuries, London; Sangallensis (S): sixth century, St. Gall; Palimpsest of Autun: 5-6 centuries, Autun.

THE "AUTHENTICITY"   The Fathers of the Council of Trent, in the
OF THE VULGATE   decree *Insuper*, declared the Vulgate to be
the authentic version among the other Latin versions. But the Vulgate itself required correction (it should be published *quam emendatissime*—"as correctly as possible"); the "authenticity" given it regarded faith and morals, not critical accuracy. The Vulgate was declared the official Bible of the Latin Church; its doctrinal accuracy was guaranteeed by the long use and approbation of the infallible Church. From the Acts of the Council it is quite clear that the theologians of the Council understood the term "authentic" in this juridical sense: "It was declared authentic or authoritative in the sense that its testimony in doctrinal matters can never be legitimately rejected. Its accuracy in other respects is neither asserted nor implied." This notion of authenticity was frequently misunderstood. Some theologians upheld the puerile assertion that the Vulgate is superior to the original texts. Pope Pius XII clearly defined the term:

> As for the decree of the Council of Trent requiring the Vulgate to be the Latin version "which all should use as authentic," this, as everybody knows, concerns only the Latin Church and her public use of the Scripture, and obviously in no way derogates from the authority and value of the original texts. . . . This pre-eminent authority, or "authenticity," of the Vulgate was determined by the Council not primarily on critical grounds, but rather by reason of its legitimate use in the churches through the course of so many centuries, a use which proves this version . . . to be entirely immune from any error in matters of faith and morals. . . . Its authenticity is, therefore, more properly called *juridical* than *critical*.[15]

While the Vulgate remains, in the sense indicated, the official version of the Latin Church, its importance should not be overesti-

---

[15]*Divino Afflante Spiritu* (London: C.T.S.), n. 26.

mated. For scholars it is just one version among many. There is no particular merit in basing a modern vernacular translation on it alone. The present-day practice—the only reasonable one—is to go back, in all cases, to the critically established original text. It is certain that a version made on any basis other than this is already dated.[16]

---

[16]For a survey of versions in English, see A. Robert and A. Tricot, *Guide to the Bible,* trans. E. P. Arbez and M. R. P. McGuire (New York: Desclee, 1960²), I, pp. 665-72.

| NINE | *Biblical Criticism* |

TEXTUAL CRITICISM
LITERARY CRITICISM
HISTORICAL CRITICISM
THE BIBLE IN THE CHURCH

From the first we have stressed the human aspect of the Bible; and it is from the human standpoint that we have, in the main, considered it. Nevertheless we have not overlooked the divine aspect of Scripture. The fundamental fact of inspiration and the matter of secondary senses presuppose the divine authorship of Scripture; indeed these are realities only for one who acknowledges a divine Author. Thus it is that the Catholic scholar can never take an entirely detached view of the Bible. He may, and must, use the scientific methods at his disposal; but he is committed to a belief in the divine message of the human words he studies. This does not make his approach any less objective: as a scholar he must deal honestly and courageously with the facts; and for him, the divine authorship of Scripture—which he accepts on faith—is the basic fact. All things being equal, he is in a better position to understand the word of God than others. This does not mean, however, that writers who take an incomplete view of the Bible have not contributed mightily to our knowledge of Scripture. The Catholic exegete is not hampered by his faith: he is enlightened by it. And in this age of *Divino Afflante Spiritu* and Vatican II the Catholic scholar is certainly not hampered by the supreme teaching authority of the Church.

But he is faithful to the Church and to the confidence placed in him only if he sees the Bible for what it is: words of God *in words of men.* He must approach his task in a spirit of scientific freedom,

102

applying to the Bible the principles of textual, literary, and historical criticism.

> Each of these disciplines has its proper method, which pertains to reason, and concerning which faith has nothing, at least directly, to say. If we scorn these rational procedures and claim to do without them, we are belittling the human means which God has adopted in order to speak to us and we expose ourselves to the danger of interpreting God's Scripture in a recklessly arbitrary fashion.[1]

Rational interpretation applies to the Bible the rules of interpretation of any literary work; only the human aspect of Scripture is taken into account. Hence the Bible comes under a threefold criticism: textual, literary, and historical.

1. TEXTUAL CRITICISM

Textual criticism investigates the alterations which may have occurred in the text of a document with a view to restoring it to its original form. The directive principles of textual criticism are the same for all sorts of writing, although their application varies with the documents under consideration, especially with the number, the variety, and the quality of the texts to be examined. As applied to the books of the Bible, its object is to *classify* the numerous variants found in the manuscript tradition and to *choose* those that have the best chance of representing the original reading. Thus we must find out how the changes in the text may have come about (*verbal criticism*). Then we must consider the value of the witnesses of each variant (*external criticism*) and the intrinsic quality of each reading (*internal criticism*). In illustrating the principles of textual criticism, we shall confine ourselves to the New Testament.

1) *Verbal Criticism*

The New Testament has come to us in many shapes and via a multitude of scribes. From the beginning, until the invention of printing, it was copied and recopied from century to century. During this long process there was time and room for many alterations in the text.

---

[1]Paul Synave and Pierre Benoit, *La Prophétie* (Paris: Desclée, 1947), pp. 373 f.; English edition, *Prophecy and Inspiration*, trans. Avery R. Dulles and Thomas L. Sheridan (New York: Desclee, 1961), pp. 165 f.

INVOLUNTARY VARIANTS There is no such person as an infallible copyist; hence involuntary variants are to be found in the manuscripts of the books of the New Testament which have been copied over and over, often by amateur scribes. Involuntary variants come about through *dittography* (the faulty repetition of a letter, syllable, word, or group of words), and its opposite, *haplography* (the writing only once of letters, syllables, and words that ought to be written twice). Part of a text, even a whole paragraph, can be omitted through *homoioteleuton*, that is, through words, lines, or parts of a phrase having similar endings: the eye slips from one to the other. Letters that look alike or are sounded alike (in dictation), may be easily confused; and, because of poor penmanship, words may be mistakenly read or copied. Other changes are frequent, but less well defined.

INTENTIONAL VARIANTS Such variants, although deliberate, do not necessarily argue ill will on the part of a scribe. "When there was any doubt about the original text—since it was desired that the actual text to be read, studied, and taken as the rule of faith and life should be perfect—the copyist, convinced that he was doing a good work, was bold in his corrections, his additions, and suppressions; and he grew bolder as his intention became purer."[2]

A common tendency was to make corrections in spelling, grammar, and style; it was a temptation that copyists who prided themselves on their command of Greek found difficult to resist. Another widespread tendency was to achieve harmony and conformity by smoothing out discrepancies between parallel texts, between passages of the Synoptic Gospels, for instance. Exegetical and doctrinal corrections are not infrequent: difficulties were explained, or were avoided by suppressions. An example of explanation is "For the unbelieving husband is sanctified by the wife" (1 Cor. 7:14)—some add "*believing* wife." An example of suppression is: "There were also two other malefactors led with him" (Lk. 23:32)—"other" is sometimes dropped.

2) *External Criticism*

This branch of textual criticism is called *external* because it relies solely upon the authority of the documents containing the readings,

---

[2]M.-J. Lagrange, "Project de critique textuelle rationnelle du N.T.," *Revue Bibliaue*, 42 (1933), 495.

rather than on the intrinsic quality of the readings. In reality, then, our modern critical editions are based almost exclusively on the authority of the great uncials. We have already remarked that today this is seen to be too narrow a basis.[3] In determining the value of a variant, the age, number, and character of the manuscripts are to be given due weight, but they do not suffice to determine, beyond doubt, the original form of any reading. Eventually, we must look to the text itself.

3) *Internal Criticism*

Internal criticism is an estimation, according to the text and context, of the intrinsic value of variant readings. While numerous rules have been suggested, it seems that only two criteria are valid:[4]

1. *On examining the text* the critic will choose that variant which offers the best explanation of all the others and cannot itself be explained by the others. The variants must be compared one by one in detail; some will quickly appear secondary; from the rest, it will sometimes be possible to single out one reading that stands as the origin of the others. Admittedly, it is not easy to apply the principle; thus a decision is always a matter of delicate judgment.

2. *On examining the context* the critic will choose that reading which best accords with the writer's special tendencies. Not only the method of the writer, his vocabulary, his grammar, his style, and his manner of quoting must be considered, but also his purpose, his ideas, his temperament. This sense of "feeling" for a writing, although not easily defined, can be of great help to the critic in his search for the original reading. Parallel passages, and the variants of these passages, must be taken into account.

This hasty outline will, at least, have suggested that textual criticism is a highly specialized art, the art of bringing a balanced judgment to bear on a text in the light of the information furnished by the manuscript tradition. It is a dedicated task, for the textual critic should combine "a scrupulous observance of all the laws of criticism with the deepest reverence for the sacred text."[5]

---

[3]See p. 92.

[4]See L. Vaganay, *Introduction to the Textual Criticism of the New Testament*, trans. B. V. Miller (London: Sands, 1937), pp. 87-89.

[5]Pope Pius XII, *Divino Afflante Spiritu* (London: C.T.S.), n. 24.

2. LITERARY CRITICISM

Once the text has been established, its meaning must be studied and determined. This is the work of literary criticism which examines, first of all, the language and composition of the text, then investigates the literary character of a book to establish its literary form, and finally decides whether a book is authentic or whether it has been retouched.

1) *The Language*

The importance of philological study of the sacred text has been stressed in *Divino Afflante Spiritu*:

> It is the duty of the interpreter, with the greatest care and veneration to seize eagerly upon every smallest detail of what has flowed from the pen of the sacred writer under God's inspiration, in order to reach a deeper and fuller understanding of his meaning. . . . He must explain the original text, for this, being the actual work of the sacred writer himself, has greater authority and weight than any translation, however excellent, be it ancient or modern. And the accomplishment of this task will be easier and more effective if, to a knowledge of languages, is added a sound skill in the art of criticism applied to the said text.[6]

It follows that a knowledge of the biblical languages—Hebrew, Greek, and Aramaic—is essential. The exegete must study the vocabulary, grammar, and style of a writing; he should take note of technical terms and should not overlook the fact that words may change in use and meaning over the centuries. The context (the link and mutual relationship between any part of a writing and those parts which precede and follow it) must be kept in mind. Indeed, a text or passage should not be considered in isolation, for it can be fully understood only in its context. The study of parallel passages, too, where such exist, is often of great help in understanding a text.

2) *The Composition*

The next stage is to try to divine the author's plan, to identify his sources, if any, and to establish his literary form. This is difficult, because no biblical writing has a table of contents or even a division into chapters;[7] none is provided with a system of reference (although

---

[6]*Ibid.*, nn. 20-21.

[7]The division of the Bible into chapters dates from the thirteenth century. It is due to Stephen Langdon (d. 1228), archbishop of Canterbury, and was designed for facility of reference. The verse division was introduced in 1551 by the printer Robert Stephen (Estienne).

certain books do mention their sources), and the literary form is not always self-evident.

ANALYSIS OF THE   This may enable us to discover the plan of
CONTENTS OF A BOOK   the author and the unfolding of his thought
or, at least, his method of procedure. There is danger here of subjectivity, of reading one's own ideas into the work that is being studied.

ONE MUST TRY TO TRACE   While it is sometimes demonstrable that
THE AUTHOR'S SOURCES   biblical writers did use sources, and is
highly probable in other cases, it is always difficult to define the extent of a writer's debt to others. Nor is it always possible to be sure that a writer has followed a well-defined source, whether written or oral. Nevertheless, this study has enormously helped our understanding of many biblical books, for example, the *Pentateuch* and the Synoptic Gospels.

THE LITERARY   We treated of this matter earlier;[8] here it will suffice
FORM   to note that the encyclical *Divino Afflante Spiritu*
has stressed the importance of determining the literary form of a biblical writing:

> Frequently the literal sense is not so obvious in the words and writings of ancient oriental authors as it is with the writers of today. For what they intended to signify by their words is not determined only by the laws of grammar or philology, nor merely by the context; it is absolutely necessary for the interpreter to go back in spirit to those remote centuries of the East, and to make proper use of the aids afforded by history, archaeology, ethnology, and other sciences, in order to discover what literary forms the writers of that early age intended to use, and did in fact employ. For to express what they had in mind, the ancients of the East did not always use the same form and expressions as we use today; they used those which were current among the people of their own time and place; and what these were the exegete cannot determine a priori, but only from a careful study of ancient oriental literature.[9]

The point is this: the biblical writers adopted the literary forms in use among their contemporaries; thus only when we know what these literary forms were can we surely interpret any given book.

---

[8]See p. 51.
[9]N. 39.

A further difficulty lies in proving that a biblical book, or part of a book, belongs to such and such a literary form. Once the fact has been established, however, the interpretation of the book or passage is easier and more assured. Conversely, failure to recognize or to admit a given literary form will lead, inevitably, to misinterpretation. Account must be taken, too, of the personal style of a writer, particularly when different writers make use of the same literary form. For instance, the cultivated style of Isaiah is not that of the shepherd Amos, and St. Luke is far more literary than St. Mark.

3) *The Origin of a Writing*

We trace the origin of a book by getting back to its author and to the circumstances in which it was written; the more we know about the author the better. If possible, we must fix the date and place of composition of the writing as well as the purpose for which it was written, and we must discover to whom it was addressed. Normally we have two kinds of evidence to go on: *external* and *intrinsic*.

EXTERNAL Quotations in contemporary or later writings may help
EVIDENCE us to identify the author of a biblical book, or at least assure us of his existence at or before a given date. In principle, external evidence carries more weight than intrinsic evidence, but the testimony has to be carefully scrutinized, first concerning its genuineness and then to determine its exact sense. The various external witnesses, taken together, form a tradition; this tradition will be evaluated according to its early origin and its constancy.

INTRINSIC This is based on an examination of the content and char-
EVIDENCE acter of a work. It may confirm or weaken the testimony of tradition. We have, first of all, the express indications of the text; but here we must beware of pseudonymity, that is, the well-known device of attributing a book to a famous personage (for example, many of the wisdom books are, conventionally, attributed to Solomon). Then a study of language and style, of historical and geographical data, and of the doctrine will help us to determine the origin of a work. The result of such a study will often be negative, that is, we shall conclude that a given book cannot have been the work of the traditional author or cannot have been written in a particular epoch.

Not infrequently, however, intrinsic evidence will confirm the authenticity of a book.

Here, *authenticity* is a technical term. A writing is *authentic* if it is shown that the person to whom it is traditionally ascribed did in fact write it; conversely it is called *inauthentic*. It should be clearly understood that *authenticity* and *inspiration* are distinct. Inspiration means that the author of a given writing was moved by the Holy Spirit—whether or not we can name that author is another matter. Thus, if it becomes clear that a writing is *inauthentic*, its inspiration is in no way affected: the eventual author, whoever he may have been, was inspired.

3. HISTORICAL CRITICISM

It is not sufficient to know the purpose and content of a scriptural book; it must be established as a trustworthy document. This is the work of historical criticism. But if a biblical writing is to be fairly judged, it must be seen in its true environment. What has been said in an earlier chapter[10] about the background of the Bible is relevant here, for this is the first aspect that should be taken into account. A book must be set in its social milieu if it is to be understood and if its message is to be correctly read.

The historian will understand the data of the text only if he has a grasp of the laws that rule human society. History is not a collection of documents nor a catalogue of archaeological discoveries: it is a sharing in the life of men of a bygone age; and despite social, economic, and technical differences men of all ages are much alike. The good historian is aware of the enduring laws of human life and is able to conjure up the conditions of the epoch he is dealing with. Hence a proper appreciation of the past demands two things: (1) that one should have worked out, by study and experience, the unchanging laws which apply to past and present alike; (2) that one has enough imagination, guided by objective data, to reconstruct the situations and problems of another age.[11]

Clearly, the task of placing a Scripture text in its proper historical milieu is not always simple. The shorter the text, the more difficult

---

[10]See pp. 21-24.
[11]See A. Robert and A. Feuillet, *Introduction à la Bible* (Tournai: Desclée, 1957), I, p. 161.

this is; hence, for instance, the wide margin of disagreement in dating many of the psalms. In order to form a judgment we have to fall back on the results of literary criticism.

> In practice, there is no rigid sequence, logical or chronological, between literary criticism and historical criticism: they are closely linked, and one sustains the other. The study of literary forms and of the expressions used by the biblical authors demands a knowledge of the milieu in which they lived; and, on the other hand, knowledge of the milieu rests in large part on a study of the texts themselves. But this is no vicious circle: it is the very condition of scientific method when one is studying the past; and the different aspects of the past—history, sociology, literature, thought—are progressively clarified, all together.[12]

For a long time our knowledge of the biblical environment was derived exclusively from the Bible itself. Since the end of the last century, however, the situation has changed radically. The change is due to archaeological discoveries which have not only supplemented biblical data, but have brought to light whole civilizations that had disappeared, apparently without trace, and a rich and varied literature whose existence was not even suspected. Indeed today we are more accurately informed concerning certain periods of world history than of the corresponding period of Israelite history. Israel is no longer seen in isolation, but plays its part on a vast stage, a part that, humanly speaking, is scarcely more than that of an extra. The result is not only a better grasp of Israel's history, but a deeper appreciation of the mystery of God's choice. We see, as never before, how exact is Israel's awareness of her true dimension: "It was not because you were more in number than any other people that the Lord set his love upon you and chose you, for you were the fewest of all peoples" (Dt. 7:7).

Archaeology is concerned both with material remains and with inscriptions and texts. The former are indispensable for the reconstruction of Israelite history; the latter, however, have thrown more light on the text of the Bible, for "nothing can eliminate the stubborn fact that the Bible is a written document and will thus be illuminated more directly by written sources, especially when they belong to the same period."[13] This is why the Ugaritic texts (several thousand clay

---

[12]*Ibid.*, pp. 162 f.
[13]W. F. Albright, *Peake's Commentary on the Bible* (London: Nelson, 1962²), n. 45 a.

tablets and fragments unearthed during excavations at Ugarit—modern Ras Shamra on the Syrian coast—and dating from between 1400 and 1200 B.C.) have shed more light on the text of the Bible than all the nonepigraphic finds yet made in Palestine. Similarly the Qumran texts have notably illustrated the background of the New Testament.

It is not surprising, then, that *Divino Afflante Spiritu* stresses the importance of archaeology and urges the fullest use of the contributions of that science.

> [In this century archaeological explorations] have become much more frequent and, being conducted by stricter methods and with experienced skill, are providing much more abundant and more reliable information. How deeply the better and fuller understanding of the Sacred Books is indebted to such investigations is well known to experts and to all those who devote themselves to these studies. Their importance is increased by the frequent discovery of written records which contribute greatly to our knowledge of the languages, literature, events, customs, and cults of very ancient times. Equally noteworthy is the discovery and examination, so frequent in our own day, of papyri, which have given us very valuable information concerning the literature and institutions, public and private, especially of the time of our Savior. . . . All these are benefits granted by divine Providence to our age, and they serve as a stimulus and an encouragement to interpreters of Holy Writ to make eager use of the great light thus afforded for a closer examination, a clearer explanation, and a more lucid exposition of Sacred Scripture. . . . To assure the uninterrupted continuance of this work and its more and more successful advancement is our object in this encyclical.[14]

The Catholic exegete is confident that the truth of the Bible will emerge triumphant from this comparison with human sources of information; evidently, an accurate notion of inerrancy is presupposed. Yet he is not preoccupied with apologetical considerations. He is aware that the surest, indeed the only way, to solve outstanding problems is to push ahead, without hesitation and boldly, the scientific criticism of the biblical text. Indeed, he must be prepared to make mistakes, to take wrong turnings, for it is only by following every line that our understanding of Scripture will deepen; and, after all, to map out and signpost a cul-de-sac is a positive achievement. All the while the scholar will be guided by his own critical faculty and by the searching scrutiny of his colleagues. Catholic biblical scholarship has come very far during the past fifty years. It is now

---

[14]Pope Pius XII, *op. cit.*, nn. 16-18.

serenely sure of itself and it seems certain that the next half-century must bring results that will dwarf the notable achievements of our own day.

4. THE BIBLE IN THE CHURCH

1) *The Church and the Bible*

While the Catholic exegete must employ the methods of rational interpretation, he must take the Bible too for what it really is, the word of God.

> An exegete who neglects the human author and the rational methods of procedure which are necessary to understand him, exposes himself to the danger of remaining on the outside of Scripture by introducing subtle and arbitrary interpretations which are not willed by God. One who rejects the divine Author and the means necessary to approach him—faith and the Church—condemns himself to remain on the outer surface of the sacred book, and even to do violence to its meaning. The exegete who takes both authors into account and maintains an exact hierarchy between the directives of faith and the demands of reason is able to penetrate Scripture in a harmonious and truly comprehensive fashion. On the solid foundation of a *scientific and critical exegesis,* which takes into consideration every human quality of the book, he will be able to erect a *theological and spiritual exegesis* which will disclose the intentions and teachings of God with the firmest guarantees.[15]

In order to achieve this desired result, however, it is necessary that the scholar be guided not only by his scholarship, not only by his faith in the divine origin of Scripture, but also by the teaching authority of a divinely-founded Church.

Christ became man, suffered, died, and rose from the dead, that all men might be saved (1 Tm. 2:4-6; 1:15); he founded his Church that men might be guided along the road of salvation. To this end, too, the word of God has been entrusted to the Church—not to be kept as a treasured heirloom, but to be the source and inspiration of the Church's teaching. The same Spirit who moved the sacred writers assists the Church in understanding their writings;[16] hence the Bible must be seen in its proper environment of a living Church, enlightened by the living tradition of that Church. And the Catholic

---

[15]Benoit, *op. cit.,* p. 168. I have transposed the order of the first two sentences.

[16]See P. Grelot, *Introduction à la Bible* (Tournai: Desclée, 1957), I, p. 199.

exegete, aware that the Church retains the supreme right to direct exegesis, will always be guided by the Church, even while he pursues his task with the utmost scientific rigor. It remains to see how, in practice, this guidance becomes effective.

2) *The Authentic Interpretation of Scripture*

The Church is the authentic interpreter of Scripture. This is a statement that must be correctly understood. It does not mean that the Church will pronounce, authoritatively and positively, on matters of criticism and on historical details if these are unconnected with dogmatic or moral issues, for the Church is concerned with questions of faith and morals and matters directly connected with them. In this context it appears that *res fidei et morum*[17]—matters concerning faith and human conduct—mean not only dogmas, but other truths that are connected with matters of faith, so that their denial would involve denial of a dogma—at least of the dogma of inspiration. Therefore, in the case of *res fidei et morum* (strictly so described), the Church has the right of interpreting Scripture positively, directly, and infallibly; in the case of matters connected with *res fidei et morum*, it has the right of interpreting Scripture indirectly and negatively, that is, it has the right of rejecting any sense and interpretation which is contrary to faith or the dogma of divine inspiration.

In fact the Church has rarely solemnly and positively defined the sense of particular texts.[18] More frequently a text is indirectly interpreted; this is done either by bringing forward a text and saying that it contains a defined doctrine or by rejecting an interpretation which implies formal error in Scripture—in these cases, however, care must be taken not to exaggerate the weight laid on a given text. The interpretation proposed by the Fathers of texts of Scripture is a principle of authentic interpretation, but only when it is a matter of faith and morals and when there is unanimous agreement. Hence *Divino Afflante Spiritu*, defending the freedom of exegetes, can admonish "all other children of the Church" that, "among the many matters set forth in the legal, historical, sapiential, and prophetical books of the Bible, there are only a few whose sense has been declared

---

[17]First Vatican Council; see Denz. 1788; cf. Denz. 789.
[18]For example: Mt. 16:16-19 (the primacy of Peter; see Denz. 1822 f.); Mt. 26:26 f. (the Eucharist; see Denz. 974).

by the authority of the Church, and that there are equally few
concerning which the opinion of the holy Fathers is unanimous.
There consequently remain many matters, and important matters, in
the exposition and explanation of which the sagacity and ingenuity
of Catholic interpreters can and ought to be freely exercised."[19] In
practice, the most useful guide for the Catholic exegete is the
"analogy of faith," that is to say, the conformity of any doctrine
or interpretation of Scripture with the sum of Catholic doctrine. The
use of this principle is most often negative, which means that any
interpretation of Scripture that contradicts the teaching of the
Church must be rejected.

3) *The Biblical Encyclicals*

In recent times the Church has intervened in the field of exegesis
by means of three encyclicals: *Providentissimus Deus* (Pope Leo XIII,
1893); *Spiritus Paraclitus* (Pope Benedict XV, 1920); and *Divino
Afflante Spiritu* (Pope Pius XII, 1943). While all are positive and
encouraging, the last, in its repercussion, is surely one of the most
important papal documents in the history of the Church. It is remark-
able for the broadness and serenity of its views and for the absolute
confidence it places on the good will and competence of Catholic
biblical scholars. Happily, it can be said that this confidence is not
misplaced, for the present reawakening of the Church, so dramatically
expressed in the Second Vatican Council, is due in great measure
to the dedicated men praised by Pius XII and to their successors.
The prominence given to *Divino Afflante Spiritu* in these chapters
is some indication of its fundamental importance.

4) *The Biblical Commission*

The Church's regard for scriptural studies found concrete expression
in the setting up of a special papal commission to foster and direct
them. The Pontifical Biblical Commission was established by Pope
Leo XIII in 1902. Its aims were: ". . . that Holy Writ should everywhere among us receive that more elaborate treatment which the
times require, and be preserved intact not only from any breath
of error, but from all rash opinions." To attain the first aim, it sees
to it, by granting academic degrees, that Scripture professors are

---

[19]Pope Pius XII, *op. cit.*, n. 49.

qualified;[20] in pursuance of the second aim it has published positive and negative norms in its various decrees.

The Biblical Commission is sometimes regarded as a retarding influence on Catholic biblical studies. It may have earned this reputation because of its stand between 1905 and 1910, during the Modernist crisis, when, quite rightly in the circumstances, it maintained a conservative attitude. But considerable time has passed since the clouds of Modernism have blown away; and it is significant, in contrast to the numerous decrees of the first two decades of the century, that the more recent interventions of the Commission have been rare, and consistently constructive.[21] Indeed Catholic exegetes cannot fail to have absolute confidence in the Biblical Commission. Its members are established Scripture scholars, men who are not only aware of the achievements as well as the problems of biblical studies, but who are imbued with the spirit of *Divino Afflante Spiritu*, the encyclical that reflects the outlook of the Commission.

Because this is true, it is important to understand how the replies of the Biblical Commission, especially the earlier ones, should be interpreted. Fortunately, the matter has been clarified recently. On the appearance of the second edition of the *Enchiridion Biblicum* in 1954, a note on this new edition was published, in German and Latin respectively, by the then Secretary and the Sub-Secretary of the Commission: Dom A. Miller, O.S.B., and Father A. Kleinhans, O.F.M. The note invites us to keep in mind two distinctions when interpreting the decrees of the Commission:[22]

1. *The date of the decrees.* The earliest decrees were issued in difficult times, during the Modernist crisis. It is difficult for us to realize the circumstances of half a century ago. Those early decrees must be understood in their historical context; the Commission cannot be held to maintain an attitude that is no longer justified. Thus, in

---

[20]In 1909 St. Pius X founded the Pontifical Biblical Institute (entrusted to the Society of Jesus) for scriptural research and for the training of future professors of Scripture. However, the Biblical Commission continues to grant degrees.

[21]See A. Robert and A. Tricot, *Guide to the Bible*, trans. E. P. Arbez and M. R. P. McGuire (New York: Desclee, 1960[2]), I, pp. 755-75, for a complete translation of all the decrees. The Biblical Commission's latest document, *Instruction on the Historical Truth of the Gospels*, issued April 21, 1964, reflects the outlook of *Divino Afflante Spiritu* and is an authentic development of it.

[22]See J. Dupont, "A propos du nouvel Enchiridion Biblicum," *Revue Biblique*, 62 (1955), 414-19; E. Siegman, "The Decrees of the Pontifical Biblical Commission," *Catholic Biblical Quarterly*, 18 (1956), 23-29.

a letter to Cardinal Suhard (1948), the Commission stated that the replies of 1905, 1906, and 1909 on the *Pentateuch* "are in no way a hindrance to further, truly scientific examination of these problems in accordance with the results acquired in these last forty years."

2. *The binding-force of a decree* is not the same when a matter of faith and morals is involved as when the question is critical and historical. In the first case the decree remains obligatory. However, the Commission has intervened most commonly in questions of critical and historical import. Here, too, the passage of time has helped to clarify many positions. Many of the decrees of the Commission are concerned with the authenticity of biblical writings. But today it is clearly seen that the question of the authenticity of a book is altogether independent of the question of its inspiration. The Catholic exegete of today who, by solid arguments, is led to doubt the authenticity of a book, is perfectly aware that his conclusion will in no way affect the question of the inspiration of the text.

The authors of the note state that, in matters where the conclusions of literary and historical criticism have no real bearing on faith and morals, the Catholic exegete, despite the decisions of the Commission, is perfectly free (*in aller Freiheit*; *plena libertate*) to carry on his research, *salva semper auctoritate magisterii Ecclesiae*. In general, then, it must be kept in mind that the replies of the Commission are juridical documents and must be interpreted as such. The replies are carefully worded; as a rule they are not put forward as definitive, but only in the light of the actual position of biblical knowledge. They are directive norms; as such they direct exegetical study: they do not bring it to a full stop.

5. CONCLUSION

Obviously, the Catholic scholar is not hampered by the teaching authority of the Church: he is guided by it, which is an entirely different matter. His freedom is so complete, and the calm of recent years has so helped him, that he has, it is true, drawn far ahead, not only of the Catholic public, but of theologians trained in a different school. The situation has been accurately described by a recent scholar:

The attitude of a large part of the Catholic public was formed during the former apologetic age. The result has been a great division among Catholics. It is only natural that there should be a lag of some years between the research of scholars and the assimilation of this research by the public. But it is not normal and by no means desirable that the mentalities of the two should be so far apart. The public demands information of the scholar according to *its* ways of thinking, and the scholar answers according to *his* way of thinking. Failing to understand, the public is often shocked. The remedy for this is not that the scholar should adopt an attitude which was, fortunately, discarded years ago. Rather the solution is for the public to reform its attitude and to realize the actual facts of the present situation.[23]

At first sight this may seem an unreasonable, even an arrogant, demand on the part of the biblical scholar. In fact, however, it is a plea that truth be recognized and prevail: there is no virtue in maintaining an attitude that has been proved false, merely because it is "traditional." At the same time, one notes with regret that another plea for sympathetic understanding and for charity can still, twenty years later, sometimes fall on deaf ears.

Let all other children of the Church bear in mind that the efforts of these valiant laborers in the vineyard of the Lord are to be judged not only with fairness and justice, but also with the greatest charity; they must avoid that indiscreet zeal which considers everything new to be for that very reason a fit object for attack or suspicion.[24]

But the admonition gives new heart to the biblical scholars.

---

[23]Luis Alonso-Schökel, *Understanding Biblical Research* (New York: Herder and Herder, 1963), pp. 52 f.
[24]Pope Pius XII, *op. cit.*, n. 49.

Appendix:

KARL RAHNER AND J. L. MCKENZIE
ON THE INSPIRATION OF SCRIPTURE

I have explained in my Preface that in presenting the doctrine of inspiration I have elected to follow one prominent modern theologian; I feel that a coherent synthesis will be more congenial and more profitable to the student. Besides, since Father Benoit has been constantly reworking and refining his theory ever since he first proposed it in 1947, we can profit from his deepened penetration of the subject. At the same time, however, I have no wish to seem to ignore the work of other scholars. It would be particularly invidious to give the impression of disregarding the important contributions of Fathers Karl Rahner, S.J. and John L. McKenzie, S.J.; hence at least a brief discussion of their theories of inspiration is necessary. I have chosen to do this in the form of an appendix for a purely methodological reason: I do not wish to complicate the presentation of a synthesis which I believe to be valid.

In my opinion, most, if not all, of the difficulties raised by Father Rahner in the first part of his essay[1] have, in fact, been met by Father Benoit, at least in his later writings. Indeed, a recent writer has asserted:

> Benoit [begins] with the concept of "inspiration," Rahner begins with the Church, and is immediately immersed in the social context of inspiration. Consequently he *does not concern himself* with exactly how God communicates his inspiration to the individual author. Thus

---

[1]*Inspiration in the Bible* (New York: Herder and Herder, 1961).

there need be no conflict between Rahner's social theory of inspiration and Benoit's individual theory.[2]

In the second place, while Rahner and McKenzie manifestly develop the social character of inspiration, the latter openly acknowledges Benoit's important contribution towards an appreciation of this aspect. There is no real opposition, then, between the theory presented in the text and those given (largely in the very words of their authors) in this appendix; indeed, since Rahner and Benoit approach the reality of inspiration from two different aspects, we may justifiably describe the views presented here as complementing the text. Fathers Benoit, Rahner, and McKenzie have contributed mightily to our better understanding of inspiration; we have much to learn from all three of them.

1. KARL RAHNER ON INSPIRATION

Father Karl Rahner's essay is divided into three parts: 1. The Bases of the Problem; 2. The Thesis; 3. Conclusions. But, first of all, he sets out his basic assumptions:

> We assume the acceptance of the traditional concept of inspiration, which is partly defined, partly laid down by the official teaching of the Church, and is partly the concept formed by the common opinion of scholastic theology. It is not our purpose to criticize this concept, nor to propose to change it. . . . We thus assume the traditional teaching of the Church as binding. The Scriptures have God as their author: he is the "author" in the literary sense of the word, because he inspired the Scriptures. This inspiration does not consist in the fact that the Scriptures have been accepted as canonical by the Church, nor that they interpret free from error the revelation of God.
>
> It would be more true to say that inspiration consists in the fact that God supernaturally illuminates the human author in the perception of the content and of the essential plan of the book, and moves him to write freely all and only that which God wants to be written. Moreover, God stands by him in order that the mentally-conceived and freely-willed work should also be properly performed. Here we can presuppose the validity and dogmatic sources of this concept (pp. 9-11).[3]

1) *The Bases of the Problem*

Father Rahner considers certain points which he regards as unsatisfactorily explained by the generally-accepted notion of inspiration.

---

[2]L. John Topel, S.J., "Rahner and McKenzie on the Social Theory of Inspiration," *Scripture*, 16 (1964), 34.

[3]Page references in the text are to Rahner, *op. cit.*

1. God is the literary author of the Scriptures, but the human authors of Scripture are also true literary originators, real authors. The human authors of Scripture are authors in no less a sense than men usually are in regard to their own writings. The notion of the "instrumentality" of the human author does not imply the instrumentality of a secretary; it is consistent with a truly human authorship, which is not diminished by the divine authorship. Now, the usual description of inspiration does not seem to preserve the full authorship of the human writer; in fact, we are given the impression that inspiration would be more perfect if man were a mere secretary. Then, too, it is difficult to conceive of two literary authors working together, not as a team, but in such a way that each of them would be the author of the whole. It cannot be that the causality of two authors, one divine and the other human, should, from the outset, aim at a single literary authorship; for, in this case, a single effect would be caused under the same aspect by two causes, which is impossible. If we say that the human author is only instrumentally an author, we would have to explain why he does not thereby cease to be a real author.

> If this difficulty is not to remain unanswered, God obviously must be in one sense author of the Scriptures, which should, firstly, leave unimpaired an authorship of the true, if analogical, kind, while at the same time not being the same sense in which man is an author, and secondly, would require and not merely tolerate the presence of a human author (p. 18).

2. The main point considered here is how an inspired writer can receive an illumination of the intellect of which he is not conscious; in other words, how the human writer can be unconscious of his inspiration and remain a real author. Yet it is correct to speak of the writer's unconsciousness of inspiration. "Illumination" means that God acts effectively in such a way that the human author's reason receives a certain knowledge willed by God, and this alone. How God achieves this remains an open question. The result of the investigations in sections 1 and 2 may be summarized:

> An activity is required of God which, while making him the literary progenitor, nevertheless not only tolerates human authorship, but positively calls for this and is also formally different from it. Such an

activity of God basically can be imagined in any manner, provided only that it but conceives, wills, and accomplishes the book by formal predefinition (pp. 23 f.).

3. How can the Church know which books (of the New Testament) are inspired? This cannot be established, it seems, for the individual books. It is not likely that writers, unaware of their own inspiration, could have revealed the inspiration of a particular book; and even if they were aware of their own inspiration it has to be shown that they have in fact revealed the inspiration of certain books. Yet, the inspiration of a group of writings is part of revealed truth and must have been known to the Church before the death of the last apostle. It is arbitrary to assert that the apostles, or one apostle, "had left behind a formal and explicit revelation on the inspired nature of the New Testament writings *in individuo,* in some statement which directly expressed this revelation" (p. 27); such a view is excluded by the complicated history of the Canon and the long hesitation about certain books. It follows that "inspiration has to be conceived of in such a manner that it demonstrates by itself how the Church knows the inspiredness of the books of the New Testament, without the necessity of having recourse to any statement about it in apostolic times that has no historical support" (p. 29).

4. What is the relationship between an inspired and canonical writing on the one hand and the teaching authority of the Church on the other hand? If the Church testifies to the authority of Scripture she seems to weaken her own authority and involves herself in a contradiction. For "what is the point of an infallible teaching authority if there is an infallible Bible? What is the point of an infallible Bible if there is an infallible authority?" (P. 31.) It seems that we have, perforce, to fall back on the Two Sources Theory: Tradition and Scripture, partial and complementary sources, stand side-by-side. Like so many modern theologians, Father Rahner (justifiably in our opinion) is sceptical of the validity of the Theory. Instead he demands that inspiration "should be understood as demonstrating from its own nature that the Bible is *the* book (not any book), and *the* source for the teaching authority and, conversely, that the Scripture is, from the beginning, the book of the Church who can testify to its inspiration because it is her book" (pp. 37 f.).

2) *The Thesis*

In the second part of his study the author proposes his thesis: Scripture is to be conceived as a constitutive element of the Church, which God has willed by the same act of will which brought into being and organized the primitive Church. Father Rahner prepares the way for the formulation of his thesis by a series of propositions:

1. All creation is the result of an absolute will of God. But, within the order of creation, the works of redemptive history are God's in some other, higher way than the works of nature; here we find the historical causality of the *Heilsgeschichte*. This historical action of God "attains its unique climax in Christ and the Church" (p. 41). Hence the Church is, in a quite special sense, the work of God.

2. The Apostolic Church is a unique phase in the historical development of the Church: it is the foundation on which the whole subsequent edifice has been, and is being, built.

> God, as the founder of the Church, has a unique, qualitatively not transmissible relationship to the first generation of the Church, which he has not in the same sense to other periods (or, rather, which he has to those only through the first). . . . The act of the constitution of the Church is thus qualitatively different from that of her preservation (p. 44).

The Apostolic Church is in an unique and eminent sense the work of God. The primitive Church must have been fully aware of her own distinct existence apart from Judaism and from all other religious movements of the time; she must have been conscious of her function of expounding her doctrine and of receiving further revelation. But since such revelation ceased with the end of this initial stage it follows that the existence of the Canon as a historical entity must be already set in the Apostolic Church.

3. The Scriptures are part—and the most important part—of the essence of the Church. The Holy Scriptures are essentially the book of the Church which she acknowledges as Scripture and which she interprets. The New Testament writers are not only organs of revelation but also witnesses of the faith of the Church, and the New Testament itself is a reflection of the life of the primitive Church. And, too, the Scriptures have that function attributed to the Apostolic Church, that is, that she is the norm for the later Church.

In this function of the primitive Church, the Scriptures are not some neutral factors introduced from outside, but part of this very function, inasmuch as the Church, her *paradosis* [tradition], her faith and self-realization are actualized in writing. By thus forming the Scriptures in herself, she addresses herself as the norm-giving Apostolic Church towards her own future and, conversely, by establishing herself as the law for all times to come, she forms the Scriptures (pp. 49 f.).

4. Father Rahner now formulates his thesis:

In creating through his absolute will the Apostolic Church and her constitutive elements, God wills and creates the Scriptures in such a way that he becomes their inspiring originator, their author. . . . The active, inspiring authorship of God is an intrinsic element in the formation of the primitive Church becoming Church. . . . God wills the Scriptures and himself as their originator. He achieves both because and insofar as he wills himself as the acting and efficient author of the Church. The inspiration of the Scriptures . . . is simply the causality of God in regard to the Church, inasmuch as it refers to that constitutive element of the Apostolic Church, which is the Bible (pp. 50 f.).

5. Hitherto the author had dealt with the New Testament only; now he strives to extend his theory to the Old Testament.[4] The Synagogue, unlike the Church, was not equipped with an infallible teaching authority; there was no infallible Church before the Church of Christ.

The Synagogue as a religious institution, distinct from the prophets who appeared from time to time, could not itself attest with certainty this inspiration and canonicity. The formation of the Old Testament could, therefore, not have been concluded before the time of the Church. . . . It is not surprising, therefore, that the Church accomplished the delimitation of the Old Testament Canon and did not take over a ready-made Canon from the Synagogue (p. 53).

If the formation of the Old Testament was completed in the New, the Old Testament Scriptures find their validity in the New. The Old Testament is not only an account of the prehistory of the Church, but is essentially orientated towards the New Testament as its completion. Hence Rahner can conclude:

We may say according to our thesis that, inasmuch as God causes the Old Testament as the definitive image of the prehistory of the Church, he inspires the Scriptures and makes them, his own as their author. In other words, because the Old Testament belongs *a priori*

---

[4]Admittedly, this is the weakest link in Father Rahner's theory; his argument is forced and unsatisfactory.

to the formation of the Church and not only of the Synagogue, as a part of her prehistory and as such remains valid forever, it can claim the same validity as the New Testament (p. 54).

3) Conclusions

In the third part of his study Father Rahner, in the light of his thesis, looks again at the difficulties he had raised in the initial stage of his work.

1. God is the author of Scripture because he has willed, and has had written, the Book which expresses the faith of that Community of salvation which he has founded. "God wills and produces the Scripture by a formal predefinition of a redemptive-historical and eschatological kind as a constitutive element of the foundation of the primitive Church, because and inasmuch as he wills and effects the primitive Church in exactly this manner" (pp. 55 f.). While pointing out that the term authorship used in regard to God and to man is an analogous concept the author adds, rather unexpectedly: "God can thus be said to be the author of the Scriptures of the *New Testament*" (p. 56).[5]

2. (a) God and man are both authors of the same Scriptures, but both authorships are not aimed at the same effect. God's primary purpose is to produce the Church; he becomes an author only because Scripture is a constitutive element of that Church. We might say that God is the author of the Church and that man is the author of the Book. Still, with regard to Scripture, we can really say that God is the principal author and that man is the instrumental author.[6]

(b) The human author is unconscious of inspiration in the sense that he does not feel himself moved to write precisely these lines or this page. But, on the other hand, he realizes that in his writing he is being "carried by that living process of the Church, believing in the Spirit" (p. 62). In other words, the New Testament writer need not be aware of the inspiration of each part of his work, but

---

[5]Italics ours, thus underlining the difficulty of the extension of his theory to cover the Old Testament.

[6]Father Rahner goes on to explain how his position differs from the traditional view of inspiration, but it will be admitted, by anyone who has studied the works of both scholars, that the "traditional" position, as Rahner understands it, is notably different from the theory of Benoit; in fact the latter is just as critical of the "traditional" position. See P. Benoit, *Aspects of Biblical Inspiration*, trans. J. Murphy-O'Connor and S. K. Ashe (Chicago: The Priory Press, 1965), pp. 36-123.

he has the general consciousness of expressing the message of the community to which he belongs. In this sense, inspiration is a conscious process.

(c) It is true that ultimately the inspiration of a writing can be known only through revelation; the question is how this revelation is to be conceived. Since Scripture was born with and of the Church, the Church has no need of the explicit revelation of an Apostle in order to be able to recognize the inspired books; she recognizes them connaturally and she can have come to this realization even after the death of the last Apostles,[7] as suggested by the history of the Canon. It may be said that the required revelation "is simply given by the fact that the relevant writing emerges as a genuine self-expression of the primitive Church. Her inspiredness is thereby sufficiently revealed" (p. 65 f.). In this context Rahner refers, implicitly at least, to the criterion of apostolicity:

> The Church, filled with the Holy Spirit, recognizes something as connatural amongst the writings which accord with her nature. If, at the same time, it is also "apostolic," that is, a piece of the self-accomplishment of the Apostolic Church as such, and recognized as such, it is then, according to the assumptions of our theory, inspired *eo ipso* (pp. 66 f.).

(d) It is clear that Scripture and the infallible magisterium cannot be in opposition since they are two aspects, or two moments, of one same supernatural reality which is that assurance which the people of God has of possessing the deposit of divine revelation. The Church, as God's ultimate community of redemption, has no successor; she is the bearer of the final revelation of God. Now the Scriptures are "the canonical exposition of the teaching of the early Church" (p. 71). The practice of the early Church is the norm of the practice of the later Church; and since the act of teaching of the primitive Church "is an act of composition of the Scripture, then it is obvious that

---

[7]The "death of the last Apostle" is not to be taken in a narrowly material sense. "It signifies the first generation of the Church, the period of her coming into being, as distinct from her continuation as a body constituted for all time. . . . [It is not obvious] that this period of the formative Church ended necessarily on the day in the calendar when the last apostle died. . . . Have we to assume it as absolutely necessary . . . that certain scriptural writings could not have originated after that day and need not only belong to the first generation?" (p. 68.)

the act of the later infallible teaching Church will appear essentially also as an act of reference to the Scripture. There is no clash between two infallibilities. . . . Infallibility of the teaching authority of the later Church is, by definition, the inerrant interpretation of the Scripture, because it includes by definition the link with the teaching of the early Church, which necessarily teaches the later Church and has expressed her teaching in the Scripture" (pp. 71 f.).

Father Rahner then proceeds—against the Two Sources Theory—to present his concept of the material sufficiency of Scripture. He makes four points:

1. "The sufficiency of the Scripture does not signify the elimination of 'oral tradition.' There can be no such elimination. The oral tradition is an essential and necessary postulate of the living and binding teaching authority of the Church, and is thus 'tradition'" (p. 73).

2. The sufficiency of the Scriptures "does not mean that the late unfolding of their meaning, which is the development of dogma, could be rejected by the individual Christian with the argument that the Bible sufficed for him" (p. 74). The Church derives her life from her own beginning, that is from her Scriptures; but precisely because the Church is a living entity that beginning cannot be an end; there is and must be room for the constant development of theology.

3. The principle of the sufficiency of Scripture does not make the facts of the development of dogma more difficult to understand.

> Which statement of a modern dogma could be demonstrated as having been taught by the apostles, handed down as such, the process of tradition being also historically traceable, without the dogma being also contained explicitly or implicitly in the Scripture? Thus the assumption of a Two Sources Theory by no means facilitates the explanation of the development of dogmas (p. 75).

4. If the principle of the material sufficiency of Scripture does raise difficulties in the history of dogma, this is due to a too narrow concept of the process of interpretation of Scripture.

> If we presuppose a less narrow concept of interpretation (which it is not our task to explain here), there will be no greater difficulty in tracing a modern dogma back to the Scriptures than by wanting not only to postulate but also to demonstrate this reference back to an unwritten oral primitive tradition (p. 76).

The essay closes with some brief but stimulating remarks on the history of religions, the literary forms of Scripture, the relationship between inspiration and canonicity, and the principles of interpretation of the Bible. It is surely not irrelevant to conclude our summary with Father Benoit's assessment of the work.[8] After he has expressed his reservations regarding certain aspects of the theory the reviewer adds:

> The positive contribution of [Rahner's] thesis is entirely acceptable: it is an excellent thing to once again place Sacred Scripture, and the charismatic intervention from which it flows, within that living history of revelation and of the people of God which receives that revelation. This concrete and dynamic view disposes of many misunderstandings, in particular regarding the last two points which Father Rahner considers: the criterion of inspiration and the relation between Scripture and Tradition.

2. J. L. McKENZIE ON INSPIRATION

At the start of his article[9] Father McKenzie acknowledges the validity of the statement that God is the author of Scripture and that the human writer is moved by him as the instrumental by the principal cause; but he says "it left a vacuum in the only aspect of inspiration which is open to historical and critical investigation, and that is the literary activity of the inspired writers" (p. 60).[10] Modern biblical criticism has emphasized the defect of the older theory of inspiration: it was too bookish. It seems to have assumed that each book of the Bible could be attributed to a single author and left no room for the exceedingly complex notion of authorship that is more the rule than the exception. It is generally impossible (notably in the Old Testament) to identify individuals as the authors of distinct books.

The idea of a biblical "book" has also suffered from oversimplification. In many cases a biblical writing is a compilation; "but even compilation is an inexact term for the complex process of growth and development of which these books are the product" (p. 61). We may describe many of these works as the reinterpretation of earlier material by later writers or we might characterize them as

---

[8]In his review of the original (1958) German edition; see RB, 67 (1960), 278.

[9]"The Social Character of Inspiration," *Myths and Realities: Studies in Biblical Theology* (Milwaukee: Bruce, 1963), pp. 59-69. The article originally appeared in the *Catholic Biblical Quarterly*, 24 (1962), 115-24.

[10]Page references in the text henceforth refer to J. L. McKenzie, *art. cit.*

the "lived" experience of Israel. But, in the long run, we have to admit that "the obscurity we find in searching for an inspired author is matched by our uncertainty in searching for an inspired book; unless we can answer such simple questions as who did what under the inspiring influence, there is much we do not know about inspiration" (p. 61).

In any study of inspiration oral tradition is an important, if complicating, factor—even though its role has sometimes been exaggerated. Almost all scholars would admit that the Bible, as we know it, began to assume written form only in the reign of Solomon (and no more than a modest portion of it took written shape during the early monarchy); all the earlier traditions, from the time of the patriarchs onwards, were formed by word of mouth. Nor did oral tradition cease when writing began. In the New Testament oral tradition forms the basis of the Gospels and accompanied their formation.[11] But oral traditions and written accounts are not the same; there is, at least, a notable difference in their transmission. If, in the ancient world, the manuscript was treated with great freedom—being frequently revised and expanded—the material of oral tradition was flexible in the extreme; we may even say that each retelling of the material was a new "composition."

> Who, then, is the inspired author, and what does the inspired author produce? We find it difficult to believe that the final redactors of the Pentateuch, for instance, were the inspired authors who compiled quite uninspired material, and no one thinks that the final and terminal editor is the only inspired author, whoever he may have been. Therefore we feel the need of distributing the charisma, so to speak, among the various men who contributed to the book—meaning the book we have. To me, at least, this has always seemed somewhat mechanical and contrived (p. 62).[12]

We must surely say that those who composed the materials used by the Yahwist, for instance, made a positive contribution—as did

---

[11] The role of oral tradition is made clear throughout W. F. Harrington, *Record of the Promise: The Old Testament* (Chicago: The Priory Press, 1965); *Record of the Fulfillment: The New Testament* (Chicago: The Priory Press, 1966).

[12] Though this closing observation would seem to be a rejection of Benoit's analogical distribution of the charism of inspiration, the continuation of the paragraph in question clearly shows that it is nothing of the sort. Indeed a feature of this article is the extent to which McKenzie is in agreement with Benoit: both are saying the same thing in different words.

the authors of the sources used by the evangelists. "Anyone who has contributed any of this [that is, creative original composition] to the Bible, it seems, deserves the charisma of inspiration more than editors, glossators, and redactors. The Yahwist and the authors of the Gospels were the heirs of a faith and a tradition, not its creators" (p. 63).

In order to explain more reasonably the distribution of the charism of inspiration Father McKenzie follows up and develops a lead given by Benoit and Rahner—what he terms "the most constructive addition to the theory of inspiration in the past fifty to sixty years" (pp. 63 f.). He means the social character of inspiration. Rahner regards the charism of inspiration in the New Testament as a charism possessed by the Church herself and not by individual writers—the Church is the real author of the New Testament. Benoit has pointed out that "inspiration is but one of the charismata by which the hierarchically structured religious community is guided. None of these charismata are properly understood if they are considered as communicated to the individual; they are primarily communicated to the Church within which they are exercised, and for which they are given" (p. 64).

There is an essential difference between an ancient and a modern author and the difference is of importance in this matter.

> I suggest that the ancient author was anonymous because he did not think of himself as an individual speaker, as the modern author does. He was anonymous because in writing he fulfilled a social function; through him the society of which he was a member wrote its thoughts. He was its spokesman, and the society was the real author of the literature. What he wrote were the traditions of his people, or the record of the deeds of his people, or the beliefs and cult of his people (p. 64).

Similarly, the oral reciter was the spokesman of the group he addressed and reminded them of their common heritage. We moderns may find it difficult to regard authorship in this manner but—if we are to understand the Bible—we must strive to understand the basic social concepts of the ancient Near East.

> The concept of the corporate personality, for example, is an important and operative idea in our conception of messianism and of the Church. In attributing the literature of the Bible to Israel and to the Church, we recur to an idea which seems merely metaphorical to us because we no longer have it in our society (p. 65).

Again, whereas the modern writer is an artist who wishes to express his individuality through his art, it seems that the ancient writer was more interested in concealing his individuality. The biblical writer wanted nothing more than to be the voice of Israel and of the Church.

> The Bible is the story of the encounter of God and man, but not of God and the individual man; it is the encounter of God and Israel which issues in the incarnation of Jesus, the New Israel and his continued life in the New Israel, the Church. The recital and the profession are the work of no individual writer; the writer writes what his society has communicated to him (pp. 65 f.).[13]

Revelation and inspiration are essentially an encounter with God; Israel expressed her experience of God in terms of the word of God which led to knowledge of him.

> Israel knew Yahweh because Yahweh had spoken to Israel. And because Israel had heard the word of Yahweh, Israel could through her charismatic spokesmen enunciate the word of Yahweh. Whether the word was spoken or written is a matter of minor importance in a culture where the spoken word is primary, as it was in Israel and in the primitive Church (p. 66).

This view is no return to the antiquated and untenable view of verbal dictation, a view based on the assumption that the word of God must be like the word of man.

> The word of God, the speech of God, signifies a direct mystical insight and awareness of the divine reality; I conceive it neither as an inner utterance nor as infused species but precisely as an expression of the divine reality. . . . Such an experience, I conceive, whatever else one may call it, as an effective movement to speak the word of God, or to write it. But I would insist once more that the spokesman of God speaks not only in virtue of his own personal experience and knowledge of God, but in virtue of the faith and traditions in which his experience occurs and without which his experience would not have meaning (p. 67).

---

[13]It does seem that here Father McKenzie has overstated his case. Can we really believe that Paul and John, for instance, merely wrote "what their society had communicated to them?" He has a much more satisfactory formulation of the same observation later, on page 67 (quoted in this summary). Of course, our reservation does not seriously impair the value of his emphasis on the over-all social character of inspiration.

Quite like Father Benoit, Father McKenzie finds that the inspiration and revelation of conventional terminology are not the inspiration and revelation of the Bible. As he understands the terms he can even identify revelation and inspiration.

> It seems to me that the distinction between inspiration and revelation is based on an inadequate conception of both, and I specify. Inspiration has been too closely identified with the individual author and with the written word; revelation has been too simply understood as a revealed proposition, and not as the word of God and the knowledge of God in the biblical sense (pp. 67 f.).

He also admits that, whereas all Scripture is inspired, inspiration is not quite the same in every part of Scripture. This is brought home to us by a comparison, let us say, of Jude and 2,3 John with the Gospels and the great Pauline epistles or, in the Old Testament, of Chronicles and Esther with Genesis, Isaiah, and Job.

> Many of us, possibly, have often wondered whether the term "inspiration" is not almost evacuated of meaning when we find we must insist that all these books are equally inspired and equally the word of God. If they are, we must be missing something very important. Is it not more accurate to say that they are indeed the word of God, but less inspired in the sense that the clarity of insight and the vigor of personal response is less in some men than in others? (p. 69.)

Father McKenzie concludes by setting the charism of inspiration in a larger framework. It is not coincidental that the charism of inspiration, like the apostolic office, ceased with the death of the apostles, for both endured only "as long as the Church possessed a living memory of the Incarnate Word, Jesus Christ" (p. 69). But the word of God is still spoken in the Church for "the Church is Jesus Christ, the Word Incarnate" (p. 69). The Church no longer writes the inspired word of God because she herself is the living word of God; while the inspired word finds its true environment only within a living Church which utters it with a resonance that is ever new.

Bibliography

This bibliography is obviously not meant to be exhaustive and has been restricted, as far as possible, to works in English.

GENERAL

(The works listed under this heading cover all, or most, of the field of this General Introduction.)

Articles in: *The Catholic Biblical Quarterly.* Washington, D.C.; *The Bible Today.* Collegeville, Minn.: Liturgical Press.

Castelot, J., *Meet the Bible.* Baltimore: Helicon, 1960. I.

Charlier, C., *The Christian Approach to the Bible.* Trans. H. J. Richards, and B. Peters; Westminster, Md.: Newman, 1958.

Daniel-Rops, H., *What is the Bible?* Trans. J. R. Foster; New York: Hawthorn, 1958.

Hunt, I., *Understanding the Bible.* New York: Sheed & Ward, 1962.

Orchard, B., editor, *A Catholic Commentary on Holy Scripture.* London: Nelson, 1953.

Robert, A., and Feuillet, A., editors, *Introduction à la Bible.* Tournai: Desclée, 1957. I.

Robert, A., and Tricot, A., editors, *Guide to the Bible.* Trans. E. P. Arbez, and M. R. P. McGuire; New York: Desclee, 1960[2]. I.

CHAPTERS ONE AND TWO

Harrington, W., *What is the Bible?* New York: Paulist Press, 1963.

Jones, A., *God's Living Word.* New York: Sheed & Ward, 1961.

Levie, J., *The Bible, Words of God in Words of Men.* Trans. Roger Capel; New York: Kenedy, 1961.

Richards, H., *God Speaks to Us.* London: D.L.T., 1963.

CHAPTERS THREE TO FIVE

Benoit, P., "Inspiration," *Guide to the Bible.* A. Robert and A. Tricot, editors; trans. E. P. Arbez, and M. R. P. McGuire; New York: Desclee, 1960[2]. I. Pp. 9-52.

————, Aspects of Biblical Inspiration. Trans. J. Murphy-O'Connor and S. K. Ashe; Chicago: The Priory Press, 1965.

————, "Inspiration Biblique," Catholicisme. Paris: Letouzey et Ané, 1963. V, 1710-1721.

————, "Inerrance Biblique," Catholicisme. Paris: Letouzey et Ané, 1963. V, 1539-1549.

————, "Note complémentaire sur l'inspiration," Revue Biblique, 63:416-22, 1956.

————, Prophecy and Inspiration. New York: Desclee, 1961.

Forestell, J. T., "The Limitations of Inerrancy," Catholic Biblical Quarterly, 20: 9-18, 1958.

Harrington, W., "The Inspiration of Scripture," The Irish Theological Quarterly, 29:3-24, 1962.

McKenzie, J. L., The Two-Edged Sword. Milwaukee: Bruce, 1956. Pp. 1-44.

————, Myths and Realities. London: Chapman, 1963. Pp. 37-82.

MacKenzie, R. A. F., "Some Problems in the Field of Inspiration," Catholic Biblical Quarterly, 20:1-8, 1958.

Rahner, K., Inspiration in the Bible. New York: Herder and Herder, 1961.

Smyth, K., "The Inspiration of the Scriptures," Scripture, 6:67-75, 1953-54.

Stanley, D., "The Concept of Biblical Inspiration," Proceedings of the Thirteenth Annual Convention of the Catholic Theological Society of America. Yonkers, N.Y., 1958. Pp. 65-95.

Topel, L. J., "Rahner and McKenzie on the Social Theory of Inspiration," Scripture, 16:33-44, 1964.

CHAPTER SIX

Benoit, P., "Fuller Meaning of Scripture," Theology Digest, 9:3-8, 1961.

————, "La Plénitude de Sens des Livres Saints," Revue Biblique, 67:161-96, 1960.

Brown, R. E., "The History and Development of the Theory of a Sensus Plenior," Catholic Biblical Quarterly, 15:141-62, 1953.

————, "The Sensus Plenior in the Last Ten Years," Catholic Biblical Quarterly, 23:262-85, 1963.

————, The Sensus Plenior of Sacred Scripture. Baltimore: St. Mary's University, 1955.

Vawter, B., "The Fuller Sense: Some Considerations," Catholic Biblical Quarterly, 26:85-96, 1964.

CHAPTER SEVEN

Burrows, M., The Dead Sea Scrolls. New York: Viking, 1955.

————, More Light on the Dead Sea Scrolls. New York: Viking, 1958.

Hervieux, J., What Are Apocryphal Gospels? London: Burns and Oates, 1961.

Höpfl, H., "Canonicité," Dictionnaire de la Bible (Supplément). Paris: Letouzey et Ané, 1928. I. Cols. 1022-1045.

Höpfl-Gut, Introductio Generalis in Sacram Scripturam. Rome: A. Arnodo, 1950[5]. I. Pp. 132-133.

Milik, J. T., *Ten Years of Discovery in the Wilderness of Judaea.* Naperville, Ill.: Allenson, 1959.

Wikenhauser, A., *New Testament Introduction.* Trans. J. Cunningham; New York: Herder and Herder, 1958. Pp. 18-61.

Van der Ploeg, J., *The Excavations at Qumran.* Trans. K. Smyth; London: Longmans, Green, 1958.

CHAPTER EIGHT

Auvray, P., *et al.*, *The Sacred Languages.* Trans. J. Tester; New York: Hawthorn, 1960.

Black, M., and Rowley, H. H., editors, *Peake's Commentary on the Bible.* London: Nelson, 1962².

Kenyon, F. G., *Our Bible and the Ancient Manuscripts.* New York: Harper, 1958².

————, *The Text of the Greek Bible.* Naperville, Ill.: Allenson, 1958.

Wikenhauser, A., *New Testament Introduction.* Trans. J. Cunningham; New York: Herder and Herder, 1958. Pp. 62-149.

CHAPTER NINE

Albright, W. F., *The Archaeology of Palestine.* Gloucester, Mass.: Peter Smith, 1960².

Alonso-Schökel, L., *Understanding Biblical Research.* New York: Herder and Herder, 1963.

Butler, B. C., *The Church and the Bible.* London: D.L.T., 1960.

De Buit, F., *Biblical Archaeology.* Trans. Kathleen Pond; New York: Hawthorn, 1961.

Steinmann, J., *Biblical Criticism.* Trans. J. R. Foster; New York: Hawthorn, 1959.

Vaganay, L., *An Introduction to the Textual Criticism of the New Testament.* Trans. B. V. Miller; London: Sands, 1937.

Vawter, B., *The Bible in the Church.* New York: Sheed & Ward, 1959.

General Index

Accommodation, 62; *see* Sense
Albright, W. F., 110, 135
Alexandrinus, Codex of, 86
Alonso-Schökel, L., 117, 135
Amphictyony, 8
Apocrypha,
  in Catholic sense, 64-65
  in Protestant sense, 64-65
  New Testament, 65, 69
  Old Testament, 64
Apostles, as authority in early Church, 68
Aquila, 95-96
Aquinas, St. Thomas, 22, 29-30, 39-40, 42, 71
Aristeas, 93
Aristotle, 30
Athanasius, St., 22, 27, 68, 97, 99
Authenticity, concept of, 109
Author,
  divine, 39-43, 54-56, 61-62, 102
  human, 39-43, 54-56, 61-62
    as instrument, 27-28, 39-43; *see* Instrument
Authority, in Bible, 38
Auvray, P., 135

Bardy, G., 94
Barnabas, Epistle of, 86
Barthelemy, D., 96

Basil, St., 70
Beatty, A. C., 85, 89
Benedict XV, 114
Benoit, P., x, 31, 37, 43-44, 46, 55-56, 58, 73, 103, 112, 119-20, 125, 128, 130, 132-134
Bezae, Codex, 86
Bible (*see* also New Testament, Old Testament),
  and the Church, 112-13
  authority in, 38
  chronology of, 16-19, 65-72
  definition of, 3
  formation of, 6-16, 21, 45, 55-56; *see* Canon, Criticism, New Testament, Old Testament
  harmony of, 60
  inspiration in, 34-45; *see* Inspiration
  interpretation of, 113-14
  languages of, 80-82
    Aramaic, 81-82, 106
    Greek, 81-82, 106
      influenced by Semitic mind, 82
    Koine, 82
    popular Koine, 82
  Hebrew, 80-81

137

literary forms in, 14, 36-38, 42,
44-45, 51-53; see Liter-
ary Forms
manuscripts of, 82-93
revelation in, 30-32
text of, 80-101
versions of,
Greek, 93-95; see Septuagint
of Aquila, 95-96
of Symmachus, 96
of Theodotion, 96
Old Latin, 96-97
Vulgate, 97-101; see Vulgate
writing of, 7
Biblical Commission, 48, 114-16
Black, M., 135
Boismard, M.-E., 91
Brown, R. E., 59, 134
Burrows, M., 134
Butler, B. C., 135

Cajetan, Cardinal, 71
Calvin, J., 86
Canon (see under New Testament,
Old Testament),
formation of, 65-72
meaning of, 63
Cantabrigiensis, Codex, 86
Carthage, Council of, 68, 71
Castelot, J., 133
Catherine, St., 86
Causality, and inspiration,
instrumental, 40-43, 61
principal, 40-43
Chalcedon, Council of, 71
Charism,
divine, 49
prophetic, 29, 34, 38
of inspiration, 38, 43-45
of revelation, 38
Charles I, 86
Charlier, C., 47, 133
Chester Beatty Papyri, 85
Chrysostum, St. John, 91
Church,
and Bible, 112-13
three authorities of, 68

Claromontanus, Codex of, 87
Codex,
Alexandrinus, 86
Bezae, 86
Cantabrigiensis, 86
Claromontanus, 87
Ephraemi, 86
Freerensis, 86-87
Koridethi, 87
Petropolitanus, 83
Prophetarum, 83
Sinaiticus, 86
Vaticanus, 86
Commentary of Habakkuk, 78
Conclusion, concept of a theologi-
cal, 62
Conquest, traditions of, 17
Copper Scrolls (Cave III), 77
Criticism, biblical
and authentic interpretation,
113-14
and Biblical Commission, 114-
16
and the Church, 112-13
encyclicals on, 114; see Di-
vino Afflante Spiritu and
Providentissimus Deus
historical, 109-12
literary, 106-10
and origin of a writing, 108-9
external evidence, 108
internal evidence, 108-9
composition and, 106-8
language and, 106
textual, 103-5
external, 104-5
internal, 105
verbal, 103-4
Cyprian, St., 70, 90
Cyril of Jerusalem, St., 67, 70

Damascus Document, 77
Damasus, Pope, 98
Daniel-Rops, H., 133
Darkness, Sons of, 77
Dating, of books of Old Testa-
ment, 7-8

D-C Books, 75
Dead Sea Scrolls; *see* under Qumran
De Buit, F., 135
Deuterocanonical Books, 64-66, 68
Deuteronomical Code, 9-10, 17
Diaspora, 66
Diatessaron, 71
Didactic Books; *see* under New Testament, Old Testament
Dittography, 104
Divino Afflante Spiritu, 27, 40, 51, 62, 100, 102, 105, 107, 111, 113, 115
Donlan, T. C., x
Dostoyevsky, F., 52
Dupont, J., 115

Editing, of books of Bible, 7, 10-11, 17
Elohist, 9
Encyclicals, biblical, 114; *see* under specific titles
Enoch, Book of, 76
Ephesus, Council of, 71
Ephraemi, Codex of, 86
Ephrem, St., 86
Epipharius, 67, 70, 96
Epistle of Barnabas, 86
Epistles, history of, 15
Erasmus, 71
Error, concept of, 47-48
Estienne, R.: *see* Stephen, R.
Eusebius, St., 67, 89, 91, 98
Evil, concept of, 47-48
External Assistance, theory of, 28

Feuillet, A., 73, 109, 133
Fidelity, Israel's, 13
Florence, Council of, 27
Forestall, J. T., 134
Former Prophets, 4, 66, 75, 83
Freer, C. L., 87

Gemara, 81
Genesis Apocryphon, 76
Gnosticism, 69

Good News, 68
Gospels, 15, 69
Greek Culture,
    Jewish assimilation of, 13-14
    Jewish resistance to, 13
Gregory Nazianzen, St., 67, 70
Gregory Nyssa, St., 70
Gregory the Great, St., 27
Grelot, P., 112
Grenfell, 85
Grollenberg, L. H., 13

Habakkuk, Commentary of, 78
Hadrian, 95
Haplography, 104
Harrington, W. F., 14, 129, 133-34
Hasidim, 78
Hegesippus, 69
Heilsgeschichte, 34; *see* History, Sacred
Hellenization, 14-15
Hermas, Pastor of, 86
Hervieux, J., 134
Hexapla, 94-96
Hippo, Council of, 68-71
Historical Books; *see* under New Testament, Old Testament
History, Sacred, 34, 49, 56
History, theology of, 13
Holiness, of Yahweh, 11
Holy Spirit, as author of Scripture, 27, 31-34, 38-40, 45, 54
Homoioteleuton, 104
Höpfl, H., 134
Höpfl-Gut, 134
Hort, F. J. A., 81
Hunt, I., 85, 133

Inerrancy, 46-53
    and history, 49-51
    and inspiration, 46-49
    and intention of sacred writer, 48-49
    and literary forms, 51-53
    extent of in Scripture, 46-48
    meaning of, 46
    not authenticity, 109

Innocent I, 68, 71
Inspiration, 20, 32-34, 38-39, 64
  and practical judgment, 36-38
  and speculative judgment, 36-38
  and revelation, 29-34
  concept of, 25-34
  charism of, 38
  Church as sign of, 64
  definition of, 35-36
  erroneous views on, 27-28
  extent of, 43-45
  external assistance in, 28
  guarantee of, 64
  J. L. McKenzie on, 128-32
  K. Rahner on, 120-28
  psychology of, 35, 45
  scriptural, 33, 35-36, 39, 46-47
  subsequent approbation of, 28
  testimony of Scripture on, 25-26
  testimony of Fathers on, 26-27
  to act, 32
  to speak, 33
  verbal, 43
Instrument, notion of, 27-28, 39-43
Intention, of writer, 48-49
Irenaeus, St., 86, 90, 93, 96

Jeremias, J., 79
Jerome, St., 27, 67-68, 89, 95, 97-
    100
Jerusalem, Fall of, 14
John Damascene, St., 71
John Hyrcanus I, 78
John Rylands Library, 85
Jonathan, 78
Jones, A., 133
Josephus, 65, 79, 93
Joshua, Psalms of, 78
Judges, Tradition of, 17
Judgment, 38-39
  practical, 36-38, 47
  speculative, 36-38, 47
Justin, St., 67, 69, 71

Kahle, P., 83
Kenyon, F. G., 87, 135
Kingship, 58
Kittel, G., 83
Kleinhans, A., 115

Knowledge, of God, 22
  biblical, 22, 33
Koridethi, Codex of, 87

Lagrange, M.-J., 104
Lake, K., 88, 91
Lamentations, 11, 12
Langdon, S., 106
Laodicea, Council of, 67, 70
Latter Prophets, 66, 75
Law, 4, 9, 15, 25, 58, 65-66
  book of the, 10
  of Holiness, 11
Lectionaries, 85, 88
Leo XIII, 35, 114
Levi, Testament of, 76
Levie, J., 133
Light, Sons of, 77
Literary Forms, 30-38, 42, 44-45,
    51-53
  apocalypse, 14
  midrash, 14
Literature, sectarian, 77
Liturgical Poems, 13
Lord, as authority of early Church,
    68
Lukaris, Patriarch Cyril, 86
Lynch, K. A., x

MacKenzie, R. A. F., 134
McInerney, T. P., x
McKenzie, J. L., 119-20, 128-32,
    134
Manual of Discipline, 77
Marcion, 90
Martin, B., 85
Masoretic text, 74, 82-84
Megilloth, 66
Melito, 67
Mercati, Cardinal, 95
Midrash, 14
Milik, J. T., 74, 76, 83, 135
Miller, A., 115
Minuscules, 85, 87-88
Mishnah, 81, 83
Montanism, 69

Nabonidus, Prayer of, 76-77
Naphtali, Testament of, 76

Nestle, E., 88-91, 98
New Testament, 3, 4
   Acts, 19
   canon of, 68-72
   didactic books of, 6
   division of, 6
   epistles of, 19
   formation of, 15-16
   gospels of, 19
   Greek versions of, 84-96; *see*
     under Bible
   historical books of, 6
   Latin versions of, 93-96; *see*
     under Bible
   Old Latin versions of, 96-97;
     see under Bible
   other writings of, 19
   prophetical books of, 6
Nicholas of Lyra, 71

Old Testament, 3, 4
   as authority of early Church, 68
   as fulfillment of New Testament,
     4
   canon of, 65-68
   commentaries on (Qumran), 78
   didactic books of, 5, 52
   division of, 5
   formation of, 6-15, 65-68
   historical books of, 5, 52
   oral tradition in, 7
   prophetical books of, 5, 17, 52
   pseudepigrapha of, 75-77
Oracles, 30
   Scriptures as, 25, 27
Orchard, B., 133
Organon, 40
Origen, 67, 91, 95, 98-99

Palimpsest, 84
Papias, 69
Papyri, 84-85
Parchment, 84
Pastoral of Hermas, 86
Pentateuch, 4-9, 11-12, 15, 17, 65-
     66, 75, 83-84, 93-94, 107,
     116
Petropolitanus, Codex of, 83

Philo, 79, 93
Philocrates, 93
Pius X, 115
Pius XII, 100, 105, 111, 114, 117
Plato, 30
Poetical books, of Old Testament,
     5, 18; *see* under Old Tes-
     tament, didactic books of
Polycarp, 69
Prayer of Nabonidus, 76-77
Prophetarum, Codex, 83
Prophetical Books of Old Testa-
     ment, 5
Prophets (*see* Former Prophets,
     Latter Prophets), 4, 9,
     65-66
Protestant, version of Bible, 5
Protocanonical books, 64-65
Providence, 13-14, 50
Providentissimus Deus, 27, 35
Psalter, 8, 18
Psalms of Joshua, 78
Pseudepigrapha, 65
   of Old Testament, 75-77
Ptolemy II Philadelphos, 93

Qumran
   Essenes of, 78-79
   library of, 74-78
   scrolls, 66, 81, 83, 111
   discovery of, 73-74

Rahner, K., 119-20, 123-28, 130,
     134
Redemption, 4
Reformation, 67
Revelation, 3, 38-39
   charism of, 38
   in the Bible, 30-32
   meaning of, 30-31
Richards, H., 133
Robert, A., ix, 73, 101, 109, 115,
     133
Rowley, H. H., 135
Rufinus, 67
Rule for the War, 77
Rule of the Community, 77
Rylands, P., 94

Samuel, M. A. Y., 73-74
Scripture
  and canonicity, 63-64
    criterion of, 72-73
  apocrypha of, 64-65
  as oracle of God, 25, 27
  canon of, 63-79
  deuterocanonical books of, 64-65
  literal sense of, 55, 61, 107
    improper, 55
    proper, 55
  meaning of,
    active, 63
    passive, 63
  protocanonical books of, 64
  senses of; see Sense
Sense(s), in the Bible,
  "accommodated," 62
  and inspiration, 61-62
  distinct from signification, 54-55
  fuller, 54, 56-59, 61
  primary (see above, fuller)
  secondary, 55-56
    conditions and criteria of, 59-
      60
    homogeneity, 59-60
    reproduction, 60
  typical, 56-59, 61
Septimus Severus, 96
Septuagint, 66-67, 75, 82-83; see
      under Bible
Siegman, E., 115
Signification, distinct from sense,
      54
Signs, 56
Sinaiticus, Codex, 86
Smyth, K., 134
Soden, H. von, 91
Sons of Darkness, 77
Sons of Light, 77
Spellings, of biblical names and
      places, 5
Spiritus Paracletus, 27
Stanley, D., 134
Steinmann, J., 135
Stephen, R., 106
Sukenik, E. L., 73
Symmachus, 96, 98

Synave, P., 43, 55, 73, 103

Targums, 81
Tatian, 71
Teacher of Past Righteousness, 78
Temple,
  destruction of, 15
  restoration of, 10, 12-13
Tertullian, 70, 90, 97
Testament, meaning of, 3
Testament
  of Levi, 76
  of Naphtali, 76
  (s) of the Twelve Patriarchs, 76
Testimonia, 78
Text-forms
  Alexandrian (Neutral), 89-90
  Caesarean, 91
  Koine, 91
  Western, 90
Theodore of Beza, 86-87
Theodotion, 96, 98-99
Theta, 91
Tischendorff, C. von, 86
Topel, L. J., 120, 134
Torah, 4
Tradition,
  Elohistic, 9, 17
  oral, in Old Testament, 7
  Pentateuch, 9
  Yahwistic, 9, 17
Trent, Council of, 65, 68
Tricot, A., ix, 97, 101, 115, 134

Uncials, 85-87

Vaganay, L., 88, 105, 135
Van der Ploeg, J., 135
Vatican Council, First, 27-28, 65,
      113
Vatican Council, Second, 102
Vaticanus, Codex, 86
Vaux, R. de, 78; see Foreword by
Vawter, B., 134-35
Vulgate, 5, 12, 26, 97-101; see
      under Bible

Walsh, L. G., x

War, Rule for the, 77
Westcott, B. F., 91
White, V., 29
Wikenhauser, H., 89, 98, 135
Wisdom literature, 6, 8, 12-13, 18

Wisdom, meaning of, 12
Word of God, 20-24, 29
Word, people of the, 21-24
Writings, other, 4, 16, 18, 65-66, 83